# INTERDISCIPLINARY TEACHING

# WHY
# & HOW

## GORDON F. VARS

NATIONAL MIDDLE SCHOOL ASSOCIATION

The name Gordon F. Vars is familiar to hundreds of middle level educators, not to mention even hundreds more of one-time middle level youngsters, for Dr. Vars has been a teacher of young adolescents and a teacher of middle level teachers for some forty years as well as a prolific writer. A founder of the National Middle School Association and its first president, Gordon has also been the Executive Director of the National Association for Core Curriculum and a Professor of Education at Kent State University.

His willingness to share his considerable scholarship and experience via this expanded monograph is appreciated.

NMSA is a registered servicemark of National Middle School Association.

ISBN: 1-56090-068-7

# Contents

# Foreword

*Back by popular demand.* This common indication of a speaker's popularity can be applied to a publication as well. Since its release in 1987 Gordon Vars' brief monograph has been reprinted many times because of the demand for it. When asked to do a second edition, Gordon readily agreed and applied his considerable scholarship to the effort. What has resulted is not just an updated version, but an expanded resource.

This monograph is as timely now as it was when first published. In fact, the increasingly strong movement to integrate learning at the middle level makes it even more timely. Certainly it will continue to fill an important niche in the growing body of literature that supports the serious efforts to integrate educational experiences.

Because interdisciplinary instruction was not a part of most teacher education programs, current middle level faculties often hesitate when asked to venture into programs which move away from the departmentalized instruction to which they had become accustomed. Yet the ultimate success of the middle school movement is heavily dependent upon the full implementation of some form of integrated instruction. This new monograph is a valuable source of ideas and encouragement for individual teachers, teams, and faculties as they grapple with ways to break away from separate subject instruction. It provides succinct information on various ways of moving toward wholeness in learning and greater involvement of students. It discusses various approaches and offers specific suggestions to guide the implementation of interdisciplinary programs.

The author has extensive experience in conducting such instruction. He writes from a practitioner's standpoint, having taught in interdisciplinary programs from the sixth grade through graduate school. This is evident from the clear explanations and ample examples incorporated. While research results are included, this publication is as much a handbook as a treatise. It will, therefore, be found in the hands of classroom teachers rather than merely occupying space on the professional library shelf.

John H. Lounsbury
Editor, NMSA Publications

# Introduction

"Interdisciplinary teaching" — what does that term mean to you? "Inter-" usually means "between," and a "discipline" is a specific area of knowledge, like physics, political science, or linguistics (not to be confused with maintaining order or discipline in the classroom, of course).

Hence, "interdisciplinary teaching" is instruction that emphasizes the connections, the interrelations, among various areas of knowledge. In its broadest sense it is designed to help students to "see life whole," to integrate and make sense out of the myriad experiences they have, both in school and in the world at large.

Interdisciplinary teaching in some form has long been a distinguishing feature of middle level education. Eichhorn (1966) and Alexander (1968) suggested that it be delivered by interdisciplinary teams. In the junior high school, which evolved around the turn of the century, the block-time or core class taught by one teacher was most common (Wright, 1949; Vars, 1992a). By whatever name or method of delivery, integration has been an accepted function of middle level schools throughout their history (Gruhn & Douglass, 1947; Vars, 1984). How can this vital function best be carried out in today's schools? This publication offers some possible answers to that perennial question.

Since the publication of the first edition of this monograph, the interest in interdisciplinary teaching and curriculum has increased exponentially. This edition, like its predecessor, is intended to help middle level educators sort out the terminology, consider alternative curriculum designs, and examine other features of the interdisciplinary approach to teaching. The monograph draws on the research and experience of the past as well as current reports from classrooms across the nation.

1

Sources of additional information also are cited to help readers tap into the expanding network of educators at all levels who have accepted the challenge to help their students make sense of the complex world in which we all live.

In the 1990s, with the widespread interest in all forms of interdisciplinary teaching, news items like the following are no longer as rare as they once were.

# Daily Times

VOL. 175 NO. 58      12 PAGES      © 1993 DAILY TIMES

## New Horizons

ss Release: Guidelines for
; a MiddleSchool Provided
inNewPublication
*How To Evaluate
YourMiddle School,*
recently released by
lle Association fills a clear
rvisor of Middle Programs,
ut the ation. He said, "The
ions are right on the money.
ha I want done — provide
middle level education in a
ion."

 Program Director of the
 Center for Middle Grades
ractive and functional pub-
d for local use by practitio
possible for amateurs to
le and comprehensive as-
ol's program. Many sample
rveys, checklists, and inter-
e included and can be used
r particular situations.
g to implement the middle
onder about how they are
 evidence to back up their
about where they are, and
of what their students and
e program. This 8 ¹/₂ X 11",
on is just what such schools
ect, and functional with its
hly field-tested, How To
*iddle School* is more that
rice tag.
are briefly addressed; each
ist of questions to consider
that topic. Topics covered

te Your Middle Level
re the Program Components
School?When Do You In-
he program? Chapters con-
ts of questions and sugges-
enting and evaluating ex-
ua and descriptions of suc-
grams.

## Hillside Middle School Engages in Kite Project

In the spring, the young adolescent's heart lightly turns to thoughts of — kites! At Hillside Middle School, the entire staff and student body are immersed in a brief interdisciplinary exploration of the theme "Come Fly a Kite!"

In science classes, students study the aerodynamics of kite flying and relate it to hang gliding and the evolution of the airplane. Social studies classes examine the history of kite flying, its origins and social significance in Asia, and early uses by scientists like Ben Franklin. English classes write poetry describing the visual imagery of kites and probe the feelings that accompany kite flying. In mathematics classes students learn how to estimate altitude in both metric and English units, using the angle of elevation and the length of the kite string. In art classes they explore colors and designs to use in decorating their kites. Health teachers stress rules for safe kite flying, music teachers encourage students to compose songs about kites and kite flying, and physical education teachers organize teams and events for the big day. Some students enlist the aid of the homemaking teacher to fashion kites of cloth, and all spend time in the industrial technology lab making a kite for the great "kite day."

It is expected that on that day even the cafeteria staff will get into the spirit and serve colorfully decorated cookies in the shape of a kite. Parents and other community members will join the fun. The local newspaper and television station will cover the event.

## Quantum Leap

**Columbus, Ohio.** "The most comp
ume ever written on the exploratory r
of the middle school." This judgr
describes the scope of this major n
lished by the National Middle Schoc
Written by veteran middle grade edu
*ration: The Totl Curriculum* will fi
empty niche in middle level literat
pages every aspect of exploration
addition to two opening chapters
essential background and rationale,
ters detailing fully the exploratory
basic academic areas, the special cor
special interest activities. Suggestic
menting and evaluating exploratory
descriptions of four successful schoc
also included.

Much more than a discussion
exploratory areas — art, music, te
this volume is an elaboration of its
exploration in its proper context, the
lum. Chapters contain extensive lis
which make evident the exploratoi
inherent in every subject, course, an
authors, both recently retired facul
the University of Georgia, have prov
will go a long way to counter the fa
which has grown up between acad
ploratory courses. This point of view
ded in the text makes this book of
tance. The hundreds of questions
throughout the text make it fully fun

Attractively presented in an 8
*Exploration: The Total Curriculum* s
NMSA members, of course, recei
count. Copies should be put in the ha
who will draw on its resources as the
experiences, whatever their particu
pertise.

What Can Be Learned from a Cas
Technology Be Used as an Evalu
Should the Evaluation Report Be V
You Make Good Use of the Evaluatic
27 pages of the monograph are cor
instru

# 1.

## Rationale

I n these days of pressing demands for academic competence, how can a school justify spending a day or two pursuing the seemingly frivolous activity of making and flying kites? Why, indeed!

First, such an all-school fun activity builds school spirit, improves interpersonal relations among students and teachers, and enhances overall school morale. An occasional opportunity for students, teachers, parents, and others to have fun together is one of the best ways to create a wholesome school climate for nurturing growth and real learning. And healthy school climate is a significant feature of an effective school at any level.

Second, many of the important "higher level" thinking and decision-making skills are practiced, especially if students are involved in the overall planning of the event. Countless decisions must be made by both individuals and groups, and consequences are immediately evident if a kite does not fly or the event is rained out and no alternative has been planned. Talk about "outcome-based assessment!"

Third, learning skills are applied in carrying out real projects: reading the history of kites and instructions for kite building; calculating dimensions and costs of materials; writing reports and expressive pieces in both words and music in addition to the many practical skills required to construct a kite, such as drawing, painting, cutting, and gluing.

Fourth, the interconnectedness of the various subjects in the curriculum is dramatized through application. Students must know and apply content and skills from several fields in order to build and fly a kite successfully. Such an interdisciplinary project shows students, teachers, parents, and community members how learning and motivation are enhanced when instruction is organized around a theme, issue, or problem.

In short, the relevance of the curriculum is enhanced significantly, especially if staff members follow through by having students reflect on their experiences through journals, small group discussions, and additional creative writing. Wise teachers know the difference between mere hoopla and meaningful educational experiences. When wisely implemented, interdisciplinary teaching lets learning come alive.

"Come Fly a Kite" is but one of countless energizing topics or themes that have been used in middle schools. Stanton Middle School in Alliance, Ohio, staged a "Beach Party" in January as a counter to the mid-winter "blahs." In class, students listened to seashells and wrote about what they heard, located famous beaches of the world, and studied beach erosion and pollution. At the culminating Beach Party, teachers served the students hot dogs and baked beans, taught them dances popular in the 50s, 60s, and 70s (to the music of the Beach Boys, of course!), and all joined in playing Beach Volleyball.

Overland Trail Middle School in Kansas has used everything from "Hats" to "Teddy Bears" to "Pizza" as themes for brief all-school interdisciplinary projects. The possibilities are virtually endless.

Critics may disparage such activities as lacking in intellectual rigor or substance, forgetting that middle level schools are populated by young people who learn best when there is an element of fun in the process. Most such all-school projects last only a few days and occupy but a portion of the instructional time on any day. They represent an interdisciplinary extension of such time-honored school observances as Presidents' Day, Election Day, Earth Day, Martin Luther King Day, or even Valentine's Day. Success with these brief units may pave the way for longer and more intense study of major issues, like protecting the environment, undertaken by individual teams or houses.

Support for interdisciplinary approaches may be found in a number of the major curriculum reform efforts of the 1990s. For example, "Mathematics Connections" are a feature of all the mathematics standards put forth in 1989 by the National Council of Teachers of Mathematics. The Commission on Standards of NCTM states:

> The curriculum should include deliberate attempts,
> through specific instructional activities, to connect ideas
> and procedures both among different mathematical
> topics and with other content areas. (p. 11)

The specific standards for grades 5-8 suggest that mathematical thinking and modeling be applied to solve problems that arise in areas such as art, music, psychology, science, and business (p. 84) and also "to the world outside the classroom" (p. 70).

A similar emphasis is found in *Science for All Americans,* the position paper that guides "Project 2061" of the American Association for the Advancement of Science (1989). They call for "explicit connections among science, mathematics, and technology that relate to their human and social aspects." In this they echo a theme long evident in the curriculum approach known as STS (science-technology-society) (Cheek, 1992).

The social studies position paper that also appeared in 1989 goes beyond "connection" and advocates "integration." The following is one of the "Characteristics of a Social Studies Curriculum for the 21st Century" identified by the Curriculum Task Force of the National Commission on Social Studies in the Schools (1989):

> To assist students to see the interrelationships among
> branches of knowledge, integration of other subject
> matter with social studies should be encouraged when-
> ever possible (p. 3).

Further arguments for interdisciplinary teaching have come from those like Leslie Hart (1983) and the Caines (1991), who point out that such approaches are more compatible with the way the brain works. They argue that the brain is a pattern-seeking organ that operates best in an information-rich environment where "interconnectedness" and "meaningfulness" are stressed. Current efforts to implement the "whole language" approach to literacy also reveals the power of teaching and curriculum that helps students to "make connections "(Froese, 1991).

Benefits such as these come from many different kinds of interdisciplinary studies and activities, not just all-school events. Efforts to interrelate and integrate the many strands of the school curriculum have a long history and are a central element of the emerging consensus on essential features of good middle level education. In *Turning Points,* for example, the Carnegie Council on Adolescent Development (1989) recommends integrating subject matter across disciplines with "themes that young people find relevant to their own lives" (p. 48).

Interdisciplinary approaches also are supported by a sizeable amount of research. In these days of strict accountability it is reassuring to know that fifty years of research and more than eighty studies reveal that students in interdisciplinary programs do as well, and often better, on standardized tests when compared with those in the usual separate subjects programs (Vars, 1991). The benefits in terms of morale, interpersonal skills, thinking, and problem solving are less easily documented, but they, too, are real. Of course, schools need to monitor the learning that takes place in any interdisciplinary project. And conducting surveys of student, staff, and parent attitudes toward such studies provides yet another valuable learning experience for students.

The arguments for interdisciplinary teaching are substantial. Implementing it successfully, however, requires skill, perceptive intelligence, and a multitude of critical decisions concerning staff, student, and curriculum organization. We turn next to some of these practical questions.

# 2.

## Approaches

Interdisciplinary programs are organized in several different ways. The degrees of curriculum integration will vary accordingly. Decades of research and experience have revealed that there are both advantages and disadvantages to each approach (Vars, 1986a).

### ORGANIZATION

**The total staff approach**

The projects briefly described in the Introduction exemplify the increasingly familiar all-school theme approach to interdisciplinary learning. School-wide observances of Brotherhood Week, Thanksgiving, Valentine's Day, the Olympics, or even the arrival of spring are by no means unusual in schools at all levels. If they are to be genuine educational experiences, not just holidays, staff members must seek ways to relate both curriculum and instruction to the chosen theme. Planning and coordinating such an activity require time and effort, both precious commodities in any school. Administrative support is essential, and some staff must be given released time for planning.

Student involvement also is desirable, perhaps through the student council, and parents may be invited to participate through their parent-teacher organization or as individuals. The larger the school, the bigger the organizational task, and the more time it will take to plan, carry out, and evaluate the event.

A drawback of the all-school approach stems from the expectation that all staff and all subject areas will be involved. Interdisciplinary topics or themes, however, are seldom equally pertinent to all subject areas, and some staff members may be less than enthusiastic, whatever the theme. Moreover, most courses of study are so overloaded that some teachers may be reluctant to interrupt their courses even for a brief period. In short, the all-school approach, despite its benefits, makes great demands on staff and may be viewed as an imposition or burden, rather than an opportunity. Its value, however, warrants its occasional use.

The logistics of conducting an all-school interdisciplinary study may be somewhat reduced if the school is subdivided into houses, schools-within-a-school, or teams. No two organizational units have to approach the event in exactly the same way; indeed, each house or team may generate its own series of events throughout the year, developing its own traditions and choosing events that appeal to the staff in that particular unit. Competition between houses or teams, if not overemphasized, may add to the excitement of an all-school event.

## Interdisciplinary teams

An interdisciplinary study or event that is undertaken by a team of three, four, or five teachers is the most frequently used approach. The typical middle grades team consists of an English teacher, a social studies teacher, a science teacher, a mathematics teacher and, perhaps, a reading teacher. When housed in nearby classrooms, assigned a block of time and given the autonomy to plan instruction for 100 to 150 students, the interdisciplinary team functions like a "mini-house" or school-within-a-school.

Sometimes these teams may include one or more teachers from special areas like foreign language, art, music, home economics, or industrial technology. Or these teachers may make up their own interdisciplinary team, sometimes referred to as the "exploratory team" in reference to their task of helping students explore a variety of learning areas.

The advantages of interdisciplinary team arrangements have been amply documented elsewhere (Merenbloom, 1986; Erb & Doda, 1989; Lounsbury, 1992; George & Alexander, 1993). Interdisciplinary team arrangements help staff members maintain their focus on the students since they are jointly responsible for student progress. Planning team interdisciplinary learning experiences is facilitated by common planning time, but it is by no means guaranteed. Indeed, Bergmann (1986) points out that team planning meetings may be so taken up with ways to deal with troubled or troublesome students that little time is left to consider interdisciplinary instruction.

Some schools mandate that every team conduct at least one interdisciplinary unit each quarter. These units may be as short as several days or extend for three or more weeks. Teams may spend a portion of each day's academic block on an interdisciplinary study, with students rotating among individual team members for the remainder of the time. For example, Figure 1 presents two alternate daily schedules once used by the 8E team at Beachwood Middle School, Beachwood, Ohio. "Integrated Educational Experiences" was the name given to the portion of the day spent on interdisciplinary units by the four-member interdisciplinary teams in this pioneering middle school.

In the Peterborough (NH) Middle School, three teachers and seventy-five 6th, 7th, and 8th graders join together several times a year in an intensive problem-solving activity. The program, called *Interface,* occupies the entire academic block for up to two weeks (Carr, Eppig, and Monether, 1986).

Of course, it is not necessary to involve all members of the team in every interdisciplinary unit. Mathematics and social studies teachers may coordinate their study of election trends, for example, while the science and English teachers carry on their regular curriculum. Harold Alberty, a leading advocate of integrative curriculum, long ago cautioned against dragging everything in "by the eyebrows" if it did not fit!

The inspiration for an interdisciplinary unit may come from a variety of sources: students' obvious interest about some topic or event, a testimonial from other teachers heard at a professional conference, an intriguing description published in a professional journal. Sometimes planning begins with the end product, an exciting culminating experience, field trip, or action project. Other decisions are made later.

Regardless of the sequence in which the plans are actually generated, sooner or later a teacher or team must consider each of the steps which comprise Figure 2.

# Figure 1

## Daily Schedule of Beachwood Middle School

| | PLAN I | | PLAN II |
|---|---|---|---|
| 8:30 | | | |
| | COMMUNICATION SKILLS LAB | | INTEGRATED |
| 9:15 | | | |
| | TECHNICAL SKILLS LAB (science) | | EDUCATIONAL |
| 10:00 | | | |
| | MATHEMATICS SKILLS LAB | | EXPERIENCES |
| 10:50 | | | |
| | ARTS AREA<br>  Cooking<br>  Sewing<br>  Art<br>  Industrial Arts | | ARTS AREA<br>  Cooking<br>  Sewing<br>  Art<br>  Industrial Art |
| 11:45 | | | |
| | LUNCH | | LUNCH |
| 12:15 | | | |
| | PHYSICAL EDUCATION | | PHYSICAL EDUCATION |
| 1:05 | | | |
| | INTEGRATED | | COMMUNICATION SKILLS LAB |
| 1:35 | | | |
| | EDUCATIONAL | | TECHNICAL SKILLS LAB |
| 2:05 | | | |
| | EXPERIENCES | | MATHEMATICS SKILLS LAB |
| 2:45 | | | |

NOTE: When IEE is scheduled in the morning block it meets for two hours and twenty minutes. Only one hour and forty minutes is spent on IEE when it is scheduled in the afternoon.

Source:   Cinemascope: A Curriculum for Pod 8E
            Beachwood, OH: Beachwood Public Schools

# Figure 2

## Steps in Planning an Interdisciplinary Unit

1. Review goals and objectives for that grade level and/or subjects.

2. Review curriculum scope and sequence. Determine degree of flexibility in district mandates, such as grade level placement.

3. Determine the type of interdisciplinary approach that will be attempted: correlation, fusion, or student-problem-centered.

4. Brainstorm themes, topics, or problem areas that: (1) fit the given curriculum, (2) are interdisciplinary, and (3) appear to be relevant to students.

5. Seek student reactions and input.

6. Select one or two themes, topics, or problem areas for further development.

7. Explore the contributions of each subject area to the unit, including pertinent content, skills, and learning activities.

8. Develop an overall framework or outline for the unit.

9. Locate learning materials and other sources. Students can help.

10. Plan procedures for evaluating student learnings.

11. Determine logistics:
    a. Time frame; full-time or part-time each day
    b. Student groupings
    c. Rooms and other facilities needed
    d. Equipment needed

12. Advertise the unit; inform students, parents, other teachers; generate curiosity and enthusiasm.

13. Carry out the unit, seeking student involvement along the way and at its conclusion.

14. Evaluate the unit.

15. Recycle.

The more students have been involved in the development of the unit, the more they will invest themselves in carrying it out. (See especially Steps 5, 9, 10, 13, and 14.)

Planning an interdisciplinary unit ordinarily takes several weeks. The Orange County Public Schools (1982) in Orlando, Florida, propose the following planning cycle.

### Planning a Thematic Unit

**Week One:**  BRAINSTORM

**Week Two:**  Develop subject area objectives by the end of the week. Combine objectives and skill areas. Produce a package of no more than four to eight objectives or skill areas.

**Week Three:** Members work independently gathering resources and developing learning activities.

**Week Four:**  Teams meet to examine and evaluate. Decide length of time to set aside for the unit. Create tentative schedule of events. Divide tasks. Utilize time for preparation.

**Week Five:**  Final schedule produced with available resources: speakers, room schedules, student regrouping, other details.

**Week Six:**  Meet at the end of the week to determine last-minute details and changes.

**Week Seven:** Now that you've established your plan...BEGIN!

In the interest of efficiency, many teams delegate preliminary planning of a unit to an individual or small committee. Team planning time is just too precious to spend working out all the details of every unit as a total group. Posting unit assignments and a tentative timetable for the year in the team planning room makes it possible for staff members to pass along ideas for activities and instructional materials as they encounter them.

It should be evident, even to those who have never tried it, that planning an effective interdisciplinary study or activity is no easy task.

It requires considerable time and energy, and demands the willingness to submerge some of one's individual preferences for the good of the group project. Reluctance on the part of any team member reduces the effectiveness of the project, whether this stems from lack of interest in that particular topic or the perception that it does not seem pertinent to the teacher's subject.

For example, in the kite activity described earlier, no mention was made of the foreign language teacher. It would appear that participation in this study by the foreign language staff might be forced or artificial, except in the unlikely event that the language happened to be Chinese or Japanese and was used to read about kite history or customs in the original language. On the other hand, a foreign language teacher might well provide the leadership for an interdisciplinary unit on the culture of a particular country or on some multicultural theme like "Our Hispanic Neighbors." Sometimes a teacher in a non-involved subject area volunteers to become a teacher aide or co-teacher in another subject area for the duration of a particular unit.

Personality factors also may create problems in any collaborative effort. Even if the group members get along fairly well together, time is required just to communicate to one another what is going on in each of the teacher's classes so that the various subjects can be interrelated. And no amount of talk can communicate the subtleties of the psychological climate that a teacher creates in the classroom, one of the intangibles that is so important to middle level students.

Despite concerns with time, effort, communication, and personalities, teaming can be and is very rewarding for both teachers and students (Erb & Doda, 1989). It really is true that "two heads are better than one," and team projects almost inevitably are more creative than those generated by any one individual (Arhar, Johnston, Markle, 1992; Lounsbury, 1992; Davies, 1992).

**Block-time and self-contained classes**

The communication and personality problems inherent in interdisciplinary team approaches, plus the amount of planning time absorbed in team meetings, lead some educators to recommend that interdisciplinary studies be placed in the hands of one teacher (Vars, 1986b). In a sense, this represents an extension into the middle school of the self-contained classroom typical of many elementary schools.

Most common at the sixth grade and below, the self-contained classroom approach gives one teacher responsibility for the so-called academic subjects, with students traveling to other classrooms for subjects like art, music, physical education, home economics, and industrial technology. Self-contained teachers may "swap" classes with other homeroom teachers, or they may regroup students from several classrooms for reading or mathematics to provide instruction in groups more similar in ability. This approach is most likely to work when staff members hold elementary certification or have completed one of the middle grades certification programs that provide some depth in two or three teaching fields.

For the best results, teachers of self-contained classrooms also should be organized into teams. Grade level teams are most common, but houses or "learning communities" consisting of several grade levels are appropriate. Here, again, subgroups may plan interdisciplinary units for the team, with each member assuming responsibility for carrying out one particular phase of the unit, such as introducing it to the students, conducting a field trip, or leading evaluation activities.

Block-time classes carry the self-contained idea into the typical secondary departmentalized schedule. A block-time class combines or replaces two or more subjects that are ordinarily taught separately. For example, a teacher certified in both English and social studies may be given the same students for both subjects in two adjacent periods. In essence the teacher has a double period block of time in which to provide instruction in the two subjects, hence the term "block-time." Other combinations may include mathematics and science, social studies and science, or any combination of two or three subjects. Like the self-contained teacher, the block-time teacher may divide the time allotment in whatever ways seem most appropriate regardless of the bell schedule that may govern other single-subject classes.

An advantage of the single-teacher approach when contrasted with the interdisciplinary team approach lies in the fact that decisions are in the hands of one person. Time is not needed to achieve compromises and coordinate plans with other individuals. The teacher knows what has been taught in English, for example, without having to ask anyone, and hence can relate it to the social studies or science lesson with ease. Moreover, a close bond often develops between students and teacher when they spend extensive time together each day. Teacher-student rapport is especially critical for middle level youngsters, who are apt to be greatly in need of an empathic adult to help them through the normal stresses and strains of the transition years. Teacher guidance is an essential feature of the special form of block-time class referred to as core, which is described later in this monograph.

The disadvantages of the single-teacher pattern derive from the multitude of subject areas and other tasks for which the single teacher is responsible, and the necessity of planning sufficient variety of content and activities to maintain the attention of the students. Elementary-prepared teachers may be more comfortable with this task, hence many middle schools prefer to staff block-time programs with such teachers. Secondary prepared teachers certified in only one subject area may not be permitted to teach a block-time class. Fortunately, the newer middle level certification programs provide teachers with modest depth in more than one field and some study in other areas.

Scheduling common planning for block-time teachers enables them to function as a team, leading to exchange of classes, interdisciplinary units, and other joint projects. To some, team planning combined with block-time gives the best of both possible approaches.

## CURRICULUM

Regardless of the way staff members are organized, there are several ways to interrelate different subject areas. Unfortunately, educators have generated a bewildering variety of names for these approaches. One recent publication (Fogarty, 1991) named as many as ten different forms of "curriculum integration," although on closer inspection several of these involve more than curriculum. Terms popular in the 1990s include *integrative, integrated, interdisciplinary, cross-disciplinary, multi-disciplinary,* or even *holistic.* Also in use are the older terms such as *unified studies, combined subjects, common learnings, correlated studies,* and *core curriculum.* Figure 3 is one attempt to sort out the terms applied to various types of interdisciplinary instruction.

# Figure 3

## Interdisciplinary Curriculum Terminology

**PURPOSE**

**Holistic** — curriculum that helps students address and unify the totality of human existence—physical, mental, emotional, and spiritual.

**Integrative** — curriculum that helps students to address and unify the physical, mental, and emotional aspects of life.

**CURRICULUM DESIGN**

**Interdisciplinary/cross-disciplinary** — any curriculum that deliberately links content and modes of inquiry normally associated with more than one of the scholarly disciplines.

### Content-Centered Designs

**Multi-disciplinary** — any curriculum in which content and modes of inquiry from several scholarly disciplines are applied to a common theme, topic, issue or problem. This is usually accomplished by either correlation or fusion.

**Correlation** — the sequences in two or more subject areas are adjusted so that students deal with the same theme, topic, issue, or problem in several different courses at about the same time. Also referred to as "parallel disciplines," "sequenced," or "shared."

**Fused or integrated curriculum** — content from two or more subject areas is blended into a new unit or course. Also called unified studies, combined subjects, "complementary," or "webbed."

## Student-Centered Designs

**Core curriculum** — curriculum focused directly on the needs, problems, and concerns of students, with subject matter and skills from any area brought in as needed to help them deal with those concerns. Sometimes called "transdisciplinary." May be either structured or unstructured.

> **Structured core** — curriculum is organized around broad pre-planned problem areas within which teachers anticipate that student concerns will cluster. The study is fine-tuned through teacher-student planning.

> **Unstructured core** — teachers do not pre-plan the content of the course, but derive it "from scratch" with each group of students through teacher-student planning. Similar to the "integrated day" concept. Sometimes called "integrative curriculum" (Beane, 1992).

### OTHER TERMS

**Theme** — a generic term for any title, topic, concept, issue, or problem that is used as a unifying focus in any of the above curriculum designs.

**Problem area or center of experience** — an aspect of human life around which student needs, problems, and concerns tend to cluster.

**Teacher-student planning** — the process by which teachers and students share in making decisions about curriculum and instruction — what to study, how to study it, and how to evaluate learning.

Note that the first two, holistic and integrative, focus on the processing of experience within each individual learner. They differ primarily in the types of phenomena to be included, with holistic extending "Beyond the Terrestrial" to the realm of the spirit (Gehrke, 1991).

The curriculum design alternatives differ in the degree to which they depart from conventional departmentalized programs, with correlation requiring the least amount of change and core the greatest.

No doubt some educators will take exception to one or more of these definitions, but they represent at least a start toward some kind of consistency in this complex and rapidly expanding field. Although middle schools often call their teams "interdisciplinary," their members actually represent subject areas, such as science or social studies, rather than specific scholarly disciplines like zoology, botany, economics, or political science. Holistic approaches, because they include the realm of the spirit, would appear to be limited to private, church or synagogue-related schools. The three approaches to integrative curriculum most applicable to public schools are correlation, fusion, and core curriculum.

### Correlation

By far the most prevalent approach to curriculum integration, correlation arises naturally out of cooperative planning among teachers, regardless of whether or not they are officially members of a team. The English teacher may schedule the reading of excerpts from Upton Sinclair's *The Jungle* to correspond with the study of the industrial revolution in history class. Students may learn how to plot data in graphic form so they can use those skills when conducting water pollution studies with the science teacher. The reading teacher may use Pearl Buck's *The Big Wave* for skill practice while the students are studying Japan in social studies. And all teachers may and should coordinate their efforts to help students improve in vocabulary, spelling, reading, writing, and other skills.

Obviously, correlation requires continuous communication among staff members and a willingness to adjust the sequence in one course to fit the sequence in another course. Unlike some of the approaches described later, correlation does not require deletion of any prescribed subject matter or skills, but merely a change in the sequence of their presentation. (See Figure 5 on p. 30) Even so, some teachers resist having to adjust course sequences, so correlation is not as widespread as warranted by its obvious benefits in reinforcing learnings and showing students how various subjects relate.

On the other hand, the previous discussion of ways to organize for interdisciplinary teaching reminds us that correlation often takes place almost spontaneously in block-time or self-contained classes, where one teacher is responsible for instructing several subject areas.

## Fusion

If correlating the subject matter of two or more courses will increase its apparent relevance to students, why not go the next step and blend or meld the two subjects into one? That is the approach implied by the terms "unified studies" or "combined subjects." Instead of separate courses in English and history, there may be a double-period class entitled American Studies. History, literature, art, music—all aspects of American culture—would be examined at the same time. The approach may be chronological or organized around themes such as "Man and Nature," or "Frontiers." In such a program English is both the medium of instruction and a focus of direct instruction in skills that are needed to learn the unit content.

An advantage of fusion is that skills are employed and refined throughout the course, not just when they happen to correlate. For example, an American studies class going forth to interview Viet Nam War veterans would need careful instruction in how to relate sensitively to people, how to conduct an interview, how to take notes, and how to synthesize their information and present it meaningfully to the class. In a well-developed fused course, students may be unable to say whether what they are studying is English or social studies or something else, but they know it is "for real." In the process of fusing courses, staff members may uncover duplications that can be eliminated and gaps that need to be filled. The new combined course may thus be a better one than either of the separate courses.

On the other hand, fusion requires considerable modification of conventional course sequences. Moreover, unless care is taken in planning, the impression may be created that English, for example, is merely a "handmaiden" of social studies, or that art is just brought in to add a little variety. Fusing two or more courses requires deep understanding of the fundamental content and objectives of the subjects combined, and some teachers may believe they do not have adequate background to carry out the task.

Many of the interdisciplinary curriculum designs proposed in the 1990s appear to be variations on the fused course idea, because they start with concepts and content of conventional subject areas. Merely rearranging conventional content may not generate much student enthusiasm; the problems of relevance and abstraction must still be resolved.

Perkins (1989) has described the difficulties in identifying "fertile themes for integrated learning." He argues that a well-chosen theme "fosters a level of abstraction in students' thinking that they are otherwise not likely to reach" (p. 75). Herein lies the challenge for middle level teachers. Abstract themes like "Change," "Dependence and Independence," and "Patterns" may work well with high school and college students, but they present real difficulties for the many middle level students who are still at the concrete level of cognitive development. Broad concepts or themes that appeal to teachers too often are "over the heads" of their students.

On the other hand, when Marion Brady (1989, 1991) proposes that students study the concept of "socio-cultural systems," he makes it concrete and meaningful by relating it directly to their day-to-day experiences in a school, which is itself a socio-cultural system. Like Brady, David Jardine (1991) would invite students to examine their perceptions of reality, seeking the interconnections that are already existing in nature. He would have students encounter a pine tree and explore, not only its ecological relations with earth processes, but their own ethical, aesthetic, and emotional experiences with that object.

Although a fused curriculum focused on social problems is bound to appear more relevant to students, it still is adult-designed and presented to them more-or-less predigested. For curriculum to be truly meaningful, it must involve the students directly in the design of both content and learning experiences. In short, it must cross the line from correlated or fused subjects to core curriculum.

## Core Curriculum

Core is a type of interdisciplinary curriculum in which the primary commitment is to help students deal directly with problems and issues of significance to them. Content from any subject is brought in as it contributes to the examination of a problem. Thus core curriculum is unabashedly student-centered, beginning with student concerns, whereas correlation and fusion are adult-designed approaches that begin with more-or-less conventional subject areas (Lounsbury and Vars, 1978).

For example, for many young adolescents, coming to terms with a changing body is a real concern. A core teacher, sensitive to this, might engage the class in developing a study of "Our Changing Selves." In addition to studying the obvious biological changes that accompany puberty (health and science), the class would examine how interpersonal relations change during this period in life (social studies), how one communicates effectively with peers and other persons (language arts), how writers and poets depict adolescence (literature), how young people may deal with their feelings (guidance), how adolescence is depicted in art, song, and dance (the arts), and how body changes affect one's performance in athletics (physical education).

In addition to helping students deal with immediate concerns, the teacher would lead students to consider the broader social and ethical implications of their changing selves, such as responsible expression of sexuality, the teenage pregnancy issue, sexually-transmitted diseases, and the like. Throughout the study, students would learn and apply all types of skills: problem-solving, thinking, decision-making, and communication skills such as reading, writing, interviewing, and gathering and displaying numerical data.

It should be apparent that the ramifications of such a study would soon exceed the knowledge of even the best-prepared block-time teacher or team. Therefore the core staff becomes a "broker of learning experiences," calling upon the expertise of other school staff members, the school nurse, parents, community members such as physicians and public health workers, and many others. Moreover, the students themselves would be encouraged to seek out possible sources of reliable information, so that the study becomes a genuine cooperative venture.

Since many aspects of such a study are deeply personal in nature, all staff must be sensitive to student feelings and values. Core staff need basic guidance skills and must work closely with the school's guidance department throughout the course of such a unit. If the school has a separate advisory program, such a core unit would inevitably spill over into group guidance or advisory sessions, as students explore the personal meaning of the ideas dealt with in the unit. Better yet, the core teacher could serve as the student advisor; personal guidance thus becomes a natural extension of the core unit. Self-contained, block-time, and core teachers have something of an advantage in providing guidance, since they get to know their students more intimately from having worked with them for several periods every day (Vars, 1989). See A. M. Vars (1986) and the next paragraphs of this monograph for further discussion of these important interpersonal relationships.

The theoretical advantages of a core curriculum are apparent from the above description. Content can readily be made personal and relevant through direct attention to real problems and issues. Students can see the value of perfecting their communication and problem-solving skills. Core represents the ultimate in integration of subject matter from a variety of fields.

On the other hand, this very integration raises questions as to whether all "the basics" will be adequately "covered." Some traditional subject matter is left out in a program focused primarily on genuine problems, and students may encounter items on standardized tests with which they are unfamiliar. Even with more than fifty years of research showing that core students do just as well as others on standardized tests (Vars, 1991), there is bound to be some uneasiness on the part of students, teachers, and parents. Educators who favor the core approach must have the courage of their convictions and continually gather evidence of student achievement to show the effectiveness of the program (Vars, 1979).

Core curricula vary in the degree to which the staff pre-plans student learning experiences. In *structured core,* teachers and other staff try to anticipate the broad problem areas or centers of experience within which student concerns are likely to cluster.

For example, self-understanding is such a prominent concern of most young adolescents that one can be virtually certain it will show up as a high priority in any middle level class. Therefore the staff would identify in advance a variety of worthwhile learning experiences and materials appropriate to such a study. Some schools "peg" problem areas to a particular age or grade level where they are likely to be of most interest. For example, an orientation study of "Getting Along in Middle School" would be most appropriate for the lowest grade in the middle school, whereas a study of "Career Planning" would seem most relevant to students getting ready to leave the middle school for the high school.

Learning experiences in an *unstructured core* are not prescribed in advance, but evolve through negotiation between teacher and students. Of course, the teacher has the final say. And teacher-student planning is guided by agreed-upon criteria, such as: the unit must be worthwhile, it must be of interest or concern to most of the students, it must not be an issue or topic that they have already studied in some depth, and the like. Core teachers and students must keep careful records of the content and learning experiences of the study and forward them to the next year's teacher as a basis for future teacher-student planning. Horizontal articulation between core class activities and other courses also is desirable. This enables specialists in physical education, art, music, home economics, and industrial technology to correlate their instruction with the core unit.

The idea of basing curriculum directly on student problems and concerns permeates the middle level curriculum first proposed in 1990 by James A. Beane. He suggests that the entire curriculum, not just a portion of it, be developed through wide open teacher-student planning. Figure 4 shows Beane's conception of a curriculum organized around themes that evolve from the intersection of student concerns about themselves and about their world. Also incorporated in his proposal is attention to personal, social, and technical skill development and to major concepts related to democracy, dignity, and diversity. Some of Beane's proposed themes are shown in Figure 9 on p. 36 and the teacher-student planning by which they are developed is discussed further in the next section.

# Figure 4

## A Middle School Curriculum

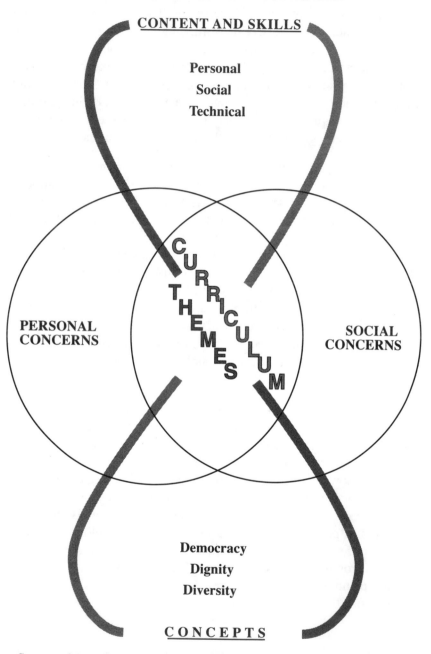

CONTENT AND SKILLS

Personal
Social
Technical

PERSONAL
CONCERNS

CURRICULUM
THEMES

SOCIAL
CONCERNS

Democracy
Dignity
Diversity

CONCEPTS

Source: James Beane (1993). *A Middle School Curriculum: From Rhetoric to Reality* (2nd ed.). Columbus, OH: National Middle School Association

## CONCLUSION/SUMMARY

In selecting ways to approach interdisciplinary teaching, schools have two basic choices of organization and three choices of curriculum design. Interdisciplinary teaching may be placed in the hands of one teacher in a self-contained, block-time, or core pattern, in which one person is responsible for teaching content from two or more subject areas; or several members of an interdisciplinary team, house, or total school faculty may be charged with the interdisciplinary planning. In this most common approach, each teacher remains a specialist in one field but contributes to a jointly-planned unit, project, or activity.

Whether taught by one teacher or several, an interdisciplinary unit may correlate content and skills from several subject areas, fuse them, or draw from those areas whatever content and skills apply to a problem that is of immediate relevance to the students.

Middle level schools may mix and match all five of these approaches. For instance, sixth graders might spend most of their day in a self-contained classroom. Seventh graders might work with two block-time teachers for English-social studies and math-science, and eighth graders might be involved with an interdisciplinary team of four teachers.

The eighth grade team may merely correlate their subjects from time to time. The seventh grade block-time teachers might fuse their subjects, whereas in the sixth grade self-contained classroom the teacher might approach core in some interdisciplinary units.

Both young adolescents and their teachers vary widely in their characteristics and needs, so schools should use a variety of approaches. Good middle schools adapt to the unique needs and characteristics of their communities and their staffs, as well as their students.

# 3.

## Planning

Interdisciplinary teaching does not just happen. It must be carefully planned, especially if the staff wishes to go beyond the incidental opportunities for correlation that come up during team or staff meetings. The type of planning required depends on how detailed the present curriculum is and how rigidly it is prescribed.

### CONTENT CHARTING

Staffs unwilling or unable to depart materially from given curriculum guidelines may nevertheless develop some exciting interdisciplinary units. One way is to first lay out in chart form the major concepts or topics to be covered in each of the subject areas to be correlated or fused. This task calls for a classroom with a large expanse of chalkboard or large sheets of mural paper. If mural paper is used, items may be written on small cards and taped to the paper so they can be moved around to match related items.

Figure 5 shows how teachers at Noe Middle School in Louisville, Kentucky, arranged the daily timetables of six different subject areas in order to correlate their study of the metric system. Note that not all subjects dealt with that topic at the same time.

Figure 6 shows a different kind of content chart, covering the first sixteen weeks of an eighth grade American Studies program at Central Junior High School, Greenwich, Connecticut.

# Figure 5

# Timetables for a Correlated Study of the Metric System

| SUBJECT | DAY 1 2 3 4 5 6 7 8 9 10 11 12 13 14 15 16 17 18 19 20 21 22 23 24 25 26 27 28 29 30 |
|---|---|
| MATH | <—— Place Value ——> <— Decimal System ——> <—— Fractions ——> <— Introduction to Metrics ——> <— Metric Linear Measurement |
| SCIENCE | |
| SOCIAL STUDIES | <—— History of Measurement ——> |
| LANGUAGE ARTS | <—— Metric Vocabulary ——> |
| INDUSTRIAL ARTS | |
| HOME ECONOMICS | |

| SUBJECT | 31 32 33 34 35 36 37 38 39 40 41 42 43 44 45 46 47 48 49 50 51 52 53 54 55 56 57 58 59 60 |
|---|---|
| MATH | <— Metric Volume Measurement —> <— Metric Mass Measurement —> |
| SCIENCE | <— Linear Metric Lab Activities —> <— Volume Metric Lab Activities —> <— Mass Metric Lab Activities —> |
| SOCIAL STUDIES | |
| LANGUAGE ARTS | |
| INDUSTRIAL ARTS | <—— Projects Using Metric Measurement ——> |
| HOME ECONOMICS | <—— Meals in Metrics ——> |

Source: Interdisciplinary Middle School Team Teaching Project. Louisville, KY: Noe Middle School, Jefferson County Schools, n.d.

# Figure 6

# Content Chart for American Studies

## UNIT 1 — EXPLORATION TO REVOLUTION — 16 Weeks

| HISTORY | ENGLISH |
|---|---|
| I. Themes | I. Literature - read one, relate to themes. |
| A. Discovery | A. *Johnny Tremain* |
| B. Colonization | B. *My Brother Sam Is Dead* |
| C. Revolution | C. *April Morning* |
| D. Town of Greenwich and Local History | D. Choose one or more books from required list for outside reading. |
| | E. Ballads of the Revolution |
| | F. Folklore |
| | II. Writing |
| | A. Assignments related to the literature |
| | B. Organizing answers to essay questions |

### JOINT PROJECTS

#### I. Biographical Sketches

| A. Research and note taking | A. Topic sentence and supporting paragraph |
|---|---|
| | B. Emphasize having a focus |

#### II. Find Your Roots

| A. Research and note taking | A. Turn notes into an expository paper |
|---|---|

#### III. Drama — Role-playing

| A. Research difficulties of adjustment for colonists | A. Write and produce own skit |
|---|---|

IV. Speakers — note taking, discussion, listening
A. Thomas Aylesworth — witchcraft
B. Jim Reynolds — balladeer
C. Jim Forrest — anthropologist

Source: Patricia Brennan and Richard Alessi (1981). *American Studies at Central Junior High School, Greenwich, Connecticut.* Kent, OH: National Association for Core Curriculum.

American Studies here is a double-period social studies-language arts program taught by an English teacher and a social studies teacher. Note that the teachers have not only charted the parallel content of the two courses but also have identified several joint projects. The balance of the year's course is charted in a similar manner (Brennan and Alessi, 1981).

Interdisciplinary units developed from charting content can tap the synergistic energy of students and teachers, while ensuring that required content and skills are covered. Tests, especially those given district-wide, may have to be adjusted because some content or skill may not be taught at its usual time. This is especially true if a concept or skill ordinarily taught at one grade level is shifted to a different level in order to fit an interdisciplinary unit. Since most course sequences are rather arbitrary, such juggling seldom makes a significant difference in student learning.

**Webbing**

In schools with somewhat less restrictive curriculum guidelines, the webbing process may be used to sketch out an interdisciplinary unit (Jacobs, 1989). A broad topic or concept is placed in the center of a large chalkboard or poster, then related ideas are added, radiating out from the center, as in Figure 7. This approach provides a graphic record of the interconnections among the various elements of an interdisciplinary unit. Teams, individual block-time teachers, and students all find this helpful. Staff may want to use different colored chalk or markers to identify topics or concepts from the various disciplines, both as a check on the balance of the unit and as dramatic evidence of cross-subject connections (Levy, 1980).

Some webbing proponents suggest that each succeeding ring of ideas have a slightly different focus. For example, after the topic and its subtopics are listed in the two inner circles, the third level may list concepts embedded in those topics. The fourth level could contain learning activities useful in developing those concepts, and the fifth level could list instructional materials useful in each learning activity. Thus a webbing diagram carries much of the information found in the typical curriculum guide, but arranges it so as to show interconnections. After the webbing diagram is completed, it can be checked against the district's curriculum guidelines to see that essential skills and content are included.

# Figure 7: Webbing Diagram for an Interdisciplinary Unit on Aviation

1. Given this weather map, calculate the chances of a storm on this flight pattern.
2. At this speed, with this plane, under these conditions, calculate the expected arrival times of these flight patterns.

1. Diagram the landing patterns one would use at these airports.
2. Design an "ideal" airport.

1. Write a report describing the effect of air pressure on the human body.
2. Write a report on survival of non-human life forms on outer space flights.

1. Write a report describing the effect of air pressure on the airplane.
2. Create a learning center explaining how airplanes fly.

1. Write a lesson on how airports are placed where they are.
2. Make a model of the surface geography of the moon.

1. Photograph the local airport, showing it in a way that is fresh.
2. Make a model of a plane. No kits please!

1. Record musical selections which show public reaction to aviation.
2. Compose a selection sharing personal experiences with aviation.

Statistics

Geometry

Biology

Physics

Mathematics

Physical Sciences

Geography

Music

Social Sciences

History

The Arts

AVIATION

Psychology

Visual Arts

Speech & Drama

Language

Non-English Language

Reading

Writing

1. Write a play about your favorite figure in aviation history.
2. Do an oral reading from a literary selection on the experience of flying.

1. Compare three memoirs of pilots.
2. Based on three fictional selections related to aviation, write a paper.

1. Write several selections of poetry sharing personal experiences with aviation.
2. Write a short story based on a person or event related to aviation.

1. Create a display on signals used to inform pilots.
2. Using the country of your second language, find out how the people of that country reacted to airplanes. Literary sources might be helpful.

1. Create a game based on your research into how astronauts are psychologically prepared for flight.
2. Write a report synthesizing quotes from pilots' biographies relating to psychology.

1. Make a time line on the history of aviation.
2. Visit the Wright Patterson Museum and share this experience with the class in an oral report.

**Source: Webbing Aids Interdisciplinary Planning,** *The Core Teacher, Vol 31,* No. 2 (Spring, 1981), p. 5

Webbing diagrams are thought-provoking and fun to develop, but difficult to store. If reduced to fit into a notebook, a fully-developed diagram is so packed with fine print as to be virtually unreadable. Perhaps the best solution is to leave it on the wall of a faculty planning room or classroom for reference throughout the unit of study, or it can be photographed on a slide and projected on a wall any time someone wants to refer to it. An overhead transparency or a computer also may be used to preserve a webbing diagram.

### Problems and issues

Even greater freedom from curriculum dictates is required if the staff is to develop an interdisciplinary unit focused on problems or issues. A unit focused on students' concerns about puberty was described in Chapter 2 in discussing core. Webbing diagrams can be used in charting a problem-centered unit, but the various rings would serve different functions. For example, the first ring around the statement of the problem could contain alternative possible solutions (hypotheses). Next would come possible consequences of each hypothesis, followed by activities useful in verifying those consequences.

Although the problems-focussed approach is certainly not restricted to core curriculum, it is so central to the core concept that its advocates have developed a way of conceptualizing this approach to education: the "problem area" or "center of experience." This is a category of human experience that embraces both the problems, interests, and needs of students and the problems confronting contemporary society (Vars, 1969, p. 8). Still surprisingly relevant today are the centers of experience proposed in 1976 by Van Til, drawing on his decades of experience with this concept. (Figure 8)

Beane (1993) has suggested a set of themes that arise from consideration of student concerns about themselves and about their world (Figure 9). Note their similarity to the Van Til list and to an even earlier list of problem areas presented by Vars in 1969 (p. 38). When it comes to life's major problem areas, each generation must deal with very similar issues, albeit in somewhat different form.

In view of the enormity of the problems included in any such list, students should not be led to believe that they are expected to *solve* the problem, but mainly to *examine* it. However, within any problem area there are many subproblems that are within the direct control of the individual or group. For example, with respect to human health, there are numerous personal decisions which must be made by each student, such as: "Shall I smoke?" "Shall I drink?" "How will I deal with my sexuality?" Many of these topics are controversial, but the school is expected to help students make wise decisions in these crucial matters based on thoughtful examination of the alternatives and their consequences.

---

### Figure 8

## Van Til's Centers of Experience

1. Self-Understanding and Personal Development

2. Family

3. Peer Group

4. School

5. Health

6. Vocations

7. Community Living

8. Intercultural Relations

9. Governmental Processes

10. Economic Options and Problems

11. Overpopulation, Pollution, Energy

12 Consumer Problems

13. War, Peace, and International Relations

14. World Views

15. Communication

16. Alternative Futures

17. Recreation and Leisure

18. The Arts and Aesthetics

---

Source: William Van Til (Ed.) (1976). *Issues in Secondary Education,* 75th Yearbook. Chicago: National Society for the Study of Education, pp. 196-212.

## Figure 9
## (Sample) Intersections of Personal
## and Social Concerns

| EARLY ADOLESCENT CONCERNS | CURRICULUM THEMES | SOCIAL CONCERNS |
|---|---|---|
| Understanding personal changes | TRANSITIONS | Living in a changing world |
| Developing a personal identity | IDENTITIES | Cultural diversity |
| Finding a place in the group | INTERDEPENDENCE | Global interdependence |
| Personal fitness | WELLNESS | Environmental protection |
| Social Status (e.g. among peers) | SOCIAL STRUCTURES | Class systems (by age, economics, etc) |
| Dealing with adults | INDEPENDENCE | Human rights |
| Peer conflict and gangs | CONFLICT RESOLUTION | Global conflict |
| Commercial pressures | COMMERCIALISM | Effects of media |
| Questioning authority | JUSTICE | Laws and social customs |
| Personal friendships | CARING | Social welfare |
| Living in the school | INSTITUTIONS | Social institutions |

Source:  James A. Beane (1993). *A Middle School Curriculum: From Rhetoric To Reality* (2nd ed.). Columbus, OH:  National Middle School Association.

After the problem areas or centers of experience have been selected for a school or grade level, it is helpful if staff members develop a "resource unit" or "resource guide" for each. These contain suggestions and guidelines to help the teacher or team develop specific learning units within that area for use with a particular group of students (Stewart, 1982; Kerekes, 1987). A resource guide differs from the typical course of study in that it includes a large number of suggestions, not just prescribed content or objectives. A fully-developed resource guide would include the following sections:

### Contents of a Resource Unit

1. Statement of rationale for the problem area.

2. Possible instructional objectives.

3. Content, often described in terms of student questions or concerns related to the problem area.

4. Possible learning activities, often classified as *initiatory, developmental,* and *culminating.* (See later section on methods.)

5. Instructional materials, sometimes classified by reading level and identified as appropriate for use by the teacher, students, or both.

6. Suggested evaluation procedures.

The format of the resource unit greatly affects its usefulness. In the past, loose-leaf notebooks and manila folders offered the greatest flexibility, but the microcomputer now appears to provide the ultimate in management capability. Years ago, Harnack (1965) demonstrated the usefulness of the mainframe computer to store and retrieve information needed to create resource units tailor-made for a particular class.

More recently, McElwain (1986) developed a system for use with the Apple II and a word processing program. Double-sided floppy disks are used which contain the district objectives for each major topic and pertinent teacher-made study guides, tests, handouts, or concept notes. The second part of the system is a set of file folders, one for each specific objective, containing materials useful in teaching that objective. These include paper copies of study guides, tests, and handouts, as well as transparencies, laboratory activities, displays, and demonstrations. The third component is another set of file folders labeled with general subject headings, in which the teacher may "dump" new reference materials, handouts, or activities collected throughout the year while awaiting entry on the floppy disk.

From the many suggestions contained in a resource guide, the teacher or team selects those most appropriate to a particular group of students. These specific plans, desirably developed with input from the students, become the "teaching unit," "learning unit," or simply "the unit." Listed below are some illustrative learning units that can be derived from a set of problem areas selected as appropriate for middle grades students.

| PROBLEM AREA | ILLUSTRATIVE LEARNING UNIT |
|---|---|
| 1. Education and School Living | Orientation to _____School |
| 2. Self-understanding | Growing Up<br>How to Make Wise Decisions |
| 3. Healthful Living | Staying Healthy |
| 4. Personal-social Relations | Achieving Maturity<br>Boy Meets Girl |
| 5. Vocational Preparation | Planning My Career |
| 6. Living in the Community | The Outlook for Teenagers in Our Town |
| 7. Intercultural Understanding | Teenagers Around the World<br>Beyond Tolerance |
| 8. Democratic Government | The Citizen's Role in Policy Making<br>Comparative Governments |
| 9. Economic Understanding | My Role as a Consumer-producer<br>Money Management |
| 10. World Problems | Surviving on Spaceship Earth<br>Ways of Achieving Peace |

Source: Gordon F. Vars (Ed.) (1969). *Common learnings: Core and interdisciplinary team approaches*. Scranton, PA: Intext, pp. 8-9.

In addition to the interests and needs of students, the teacher also must keep in mind the goals set by the team or the school. For example, as Earth Day approaches, issues related to preserving the environment could be brought out wherever appropriate in all classes. A school-wide effort to reduce drug abuse would lead all staff to stress learning experiences that build self-esteem and reverence for life. A team striving to help students reduce sexist attitudes would select learning experiences that promote acceptance of people as unique persons.

A problem-centered interdisciplinary unit is virtually guaranteed to generate student involvement, since by definition it is directed at an issue that is meaningful to most young people. Relevance is further increased if students are invited to suggest specific problems or issues for study. They often invest great energy in seeking answers to their questions, and they can see immediately the applicability of the skills of learning.

However, the problems-focussed approach is a radical departure from what most students, teachers, and parents are familiar with, so administrators and teachers must be prepared to do a great deal of explaining.

## Teacher-student planning

Teacher-student planning is the process whereby students and teachers jointly arrive at decisions affecting the conduct of the class. It is applicable in all subjects and at all levels. An elementary teacher uses it when inviting the students to help decide whether to have spelling before or after lunch. A high school teacher uses it in working out with a class the details of a field trip. A middle grades teacher uses teacher-student planning to select specific questions or issues to be studied from within a given problem area. Teams invite students to share in selecting thematic units and even the means used to evaluate student progress. Note that these are all joint decisions, not dictation by either the students or the teacher.

Even when the general boundaries of an interdisciplinary unit have been set by selecting a certain problem area, no two groups of students are likely to have the same interests and needs, and hence units developed through teacher-student planning vary considerably from class to class.

For example, one class developing a unit within the problem area of "self-understanding" might choose to explore the pros and cons of meditation or journal-keeping as a means of "getting in touch with self." Another class in the same school might have little interest in this but instead get deeply involved in discussing personal values and how they influence individual choices. Both classes would, of course, have common experiences designed to teach them the facts of human development, elements of psychology, and human nature.

Sometimes interdisciplinary units are developed "from scratch" through teacher-student planning, the "unstructured core" approach. Here there are no prescribed content guidelines, not even designated problem areas. Short term school-wide or team thematic units are often of this variety, as are some core units. Teacher and students are free to develop virtually any unit of study that is meaningful to them. Of course, the teacher is still the responsible, guiding professional, skilled in listening to and guiding student thinking. And even wide-open planning operates within certain guidelines. For example, both teacher and students must agree that the study would be worthwhile. Still applicable today are the following criteria that were established by a ninth grade core class in Maryland (Van Til, Vars, and Lounsbury, 1967, p. 261).

### Criteria for Selecting a Unit

1.  It should be within our level of understanding.

2.  It should be of interest to nearly everyone.

3.  There should be sufficient instructional materials to supply the information we need.

4.  There should be plenty of field trips, experiments, and other student activities.

5.  It should be neither too long nor too short—about six to eight weeks.

6.  It should be helpful and worthwhile.

7.  The subject should be one with which we are not already familiar.

## A unit on the future

A teacher-student planned unit on "Living in the Future" was recently reported by Brodhagen, Weilbacher, and Beane (1992). It was carried out with eighth grade students at Marquette Middle School in Madison, Wisconsin. First the students listed questions and concerns they had about themselves and also about the world they live in. Broad themes were drawn from these lists, from which the unit on the future was chosen for class study. Then students listed specific questions related to the theme, plus a long list of possible learning activities. Students and teachers next identified the knowledge and skills they would need to carry out those learning activities, demonstrating that they would be practicing and refining both the traditional basic skills and various higher level thinking skills.

One activity that extended throughout the unit was the "Madison 2020 Project," envisioning what the city would look like at that future date. The class later shared their ideas with a professional city planner. Other activities included a survey of students in seven other middle schools about their forecasts for the future and a study of life spans of family members with implications for personal health care. Student speculations as to what each might look like as an adult culminated in a visit by an artist, who made a sketch of each person in the group. Both students and teachers participated in evaluation of individual student progress and of the success of the unit as a whole.

Seventh grade students under the guidance of Brodhagen and Beane are shown engaged in a similar process in the videotape produced in 1992 by Wisconsin Public Television (Beane, 1992). In this case, the theme chosen was "Mysteries," revolving around questions about ghosts, the "purpose" of time, whether plants can think, and other aspects of reality.

Units developed through wide-open teacher-student planning represent the ultimate in student-centered curriculum. Student input virtually guarantees motivation to learn, yet teacher guidance is clearly in evidence.

Drawbacks of this approach lie primarily in the difficulty of determining curriculum scope and sequence in advance. For that reason, some schools prefer the "structured core" design, with scope and sequence defined in terms of broad problem areas. Teacher-student planning is then used to identify questions and learning activities most meaningful to a particular class.

## Accountability

Another problem becomes especially acute in these days of strict accountability and increasing state and national curriculum mandates. That is, how can one guarantee that prescribed content and skills are "covered" if the course or unit is developed cooperatively with the students?

One way is to present students with these "nonnegotiables" before beginning teacher-student planning, so that they, too, are aware of the outcomes expected. Students may prove even more creative than teachers in devising ways to meet these mandates and still develop learning experiences meaningful to them. An alternative is for the teachers to examine the theme and learning activities proposed by the class and select those that best incorporate district objectives.

Instructional materials adaptable to a student-centered core approach are virtually nonexistent. Yet even this drawback is giving way to modern hypermedia, wherein students use computers to access information on demand and in the form and sequence most meaningful to them. And inviting students, parents, and other community members to join in the search for knowledge reaps benefits for all. The day of the single textbook is long since past, especially in classrooms engaged in teacher-student-planned learning experiences.

The value of teacher-student planning has been amply demonstrated at all school levels, but too often it is limited to extra-curricular areas. Teachers and students jointly planning a field day or school newspaper carry out many of the decision-making and information-gathering skills teachers hope to develop in any classroom. Moreover, the consequences of their decisions are concretely evident when the field day or newspaper is completed. Similar processes applied to the "academic" aspect of school life yield similar benefits.

Unfortunately, teachers too often underestimate the ability of students to contribute intelligently to educational decisions, thus depriving them of invaluable experiences. Of course, the degree of student involvement must be adapted to the maturity of the students, but learning is best when teachers allow students to experience some of the consequences of ill-considered plans.

Skill in cooperative decision-making is still a rarity among adults but is increasingly being sought in modern workers. It behooves educators, therefore, to provide students with as much practice as possible.

## CONCLUSION/SUMMARY

Four basic approaches to planning interdisciplinary units have been described briefly. They vary in the extent to which they depart from the prescribed curriculum. Content charting makes it possible to build an interdisciplinary unit by merely rearranging items from existing curricula. Webbing is guided brainstorming, with the product being modified later to incorporate critical content and skills from existing courses of study. The problem-centered unit is designed around the internal logic of a problem or issue, and may omit some conventional content or skills that are not pertinent to the problem. Wide open teacher-student planning leads to units that may depart even further from prescribed content and skills, making up in student motivation and depth of learning for whatever they lack in coverage of traditional content.

These four approaches are not mutually exclusive, of course, and teachers or teams may use all four in the course of one year. Perhaps they might start with a tightly structured unit based on content charting and end the year with a brief free choice unit developed through teacher-student planning. Students who progress through such experiences gain valuable lessons in assuming responsibility for their own learning, not to mention the thinking and learning skills they develop.

# 4.

## Methods

**M**ethods used to teach interdisciplinary units arc not unique, but certain ones seem especially applicable. Teacher-student planning and small group work, for example, can be used by any teacher, yet one can hardly conceive of a thematic unit that did not employ both of these methods extensively. In the explanation that follows, only those methods or techniques that seem most pertinent to interdisciplinary teaching will be discussed.

### ENVIRONMENT

Although seldom considered a method, the classroom environment itself most certainly "teaches." Good teachers know full well the merits of a classroom filled with intriguing artifacts, challenging quotations, posters, art works, and living things. Sometimes, however, middle level teachers become too preoccupied with covering subject matter to give adequate attention to the classroom environment. Besides, middle level students may now seem unwilling to spend their time creating bulletin boards or decorating the room for the teacher. The latter phrase is probably the key to the problem — "for the teacher." However, middle level students will join *with* the teacher and other students to create an environment conducive to learning by all who occupy that room. Sometimes a thematic unit will lead to major, though temporary, alteration of the classroom environment such as the construction of an Egyptian tomb (Stromberg and Smith, 1987).

In another example, several weeks before the opening of school, a middle level teacher in Kentucky would work with several volunteers from the previous year's class to decorate the classroom. Posters were prepared and hung — not just for decoration but to communicate important concepts or procedures to the new students. Everything was designed around the year's interdisciplinary theme, be it "Roots and Wings: Security and Freedom," or "Shifting Gears" or "Lines of Communication; Lines of Relationship." Objects were even hung from the ceiling. One year it was every conceivable kind of gear or gear-driven gadget. Another year there were more than sixty living green plants, one for each member of the two core classes that met in that room. It was obvious to students from the moment they entered the classroom that exciting learning would take place and that they would definitely be part of the action. Students also knew that at the end of the year they would have the opportunity, using a different theme, to help the teacher prepare another inviting and stimulating environment for the next year's students. This inscription near the entrance made the message clear: "This room has been prepared for you, with love, by Mrs. M. and the following last year's students..."

Even more important than the physical environment is the social-emotional environment. A climate of mutual acceptance and trust must be established, culminating in a relationship that can only be called *love* (Vars, A.M., 1986).

Key to this relationship is the teacher's demonstration of three approaches that Rogers identified first within a counseling relationship and later extended into other "helping relationships" such as teaching (Rogers, 1968). Over the years, Rogers has used different terms to describe these approaches. The first is "realness," "genuineness," or "congruence," which means that the teacher's thoughts, feelings, and behavior are "in sync." The opposite of this is the teacher with the phony smile that hides dislike of children or resentment at the routines of teaching. Such mixed messages confuse students and reduce the teacher's effectiveness. Second is "prizing," "acceptance," "trust," or "unconditional positive regard." This simply means that the teacher cares about the student and affirms the student's right to control his or her own destiny. Finally, "empathic understanding" refers to the teacher's efforts to view the situation and even life itself from the student's point of view — to "walk a mile in the other person's moccasins," to quote an old Indian maxim.

While no one is expected to demonstrate all of these approaches perfectly all the time, teachers, parents, counselors, ministers, and others are most effective in helping and teaching when they practice all three. Research summarized years ago by Aspy and Roebuck (1977) amply demonstrated that teacher-student relationships built on these concepts are not only more satisfying to teachers and students, but that they also result in higher student achievement.

Methods like teacher-student planning and small group work demonstrate that students are valued as people of worth. Stanford's book, *Developing Effective Classroom Groups* (1977), remains one of the best guides for teachers seeking practical advice on how to establish productive relationships among teachers and students.

## STUDENT INVOLVEMENT

Student involvement in the learning process is essential, regardless of the degree to which student input is solicited in determining the content of an interdisciplinary unit. As a general rule, the more the student involvement, consistent with the maturity of the student, the greater the learning. Of course, that involvement must be wisely managed. Research on cooperative learning demonstrates that just putting students into small groups will not necessarily lead to greater learning of either academic content or interpersonal skills (Slavin, 1991; Johnson and Johnson, 1987).

Effective ways to guide student involvement were pioneered in the 1930s and 40s. Figure 10 illustrates the stages that a unit may go through if the teacher strives for optimum student involvement. Most of the steps are self-explanatory, but several will be amplified in following sections. The figure presumes that the unit is being guided by one teacher, but the procedures are equally applicable to an interdisciplinary team.

Learning activities carried out in these twelve steps may be classified according to the positions they occupy in the evolution of a unit: *Initiatory activities* (Steps 1-4) are designed to launch the unit and get it off to a good start. *Developmental activities* (Steps 5-9) involve students in exploring the topic or examining the issue. *Culminating activities* (Steps 10-12) wrap up the unit and reinforce the major learnings.

## Figure 10
## A Process for Conducting a
## Problem-Centered Unit

1.  **Design the unit**

    Tune into your students' interests and concerns. Invite them
    to share in designing the unit or in fine-tuning a pre-planned
    unit. Make it as relevant to students as possible.

2.  **Introduce the unit**

    The teacher introduces the unit in such a way that the
    students are motivated, inspired, challenged. The overview
    should whet their appetites, raise questions, and relate the
    unit to previous learnings.

3.  **Engage students**

    Individually, students browse through written materials,
    explore, identify resources, gather information, and list
    questions and concerns.

4.  **Develop problems through class discussion.**

    Through teacher-pupil planning identify interesting problems
    and sub-problems along with appropriate questions. Com-
    bine and narrow the list to yield five or six topics that will be
    the basis for group work.

5.  **Form groups**

    Divide the class into five or six groups or committees,
    perhaps based on their topic preferences. Assign each group
    one of the problem/topics. Assist groups in developing good
    relationships and accepting responsibility for the study.

6.  **Groups plan their procedure**

    Members discuss their topic, refine questions, consider
    research resources, make assignments, and generally plan
    how they will seek answers to their questions.

7. **Groups engage in research and study**

   Members individually or in concert with others carry out their plan, read, interview, engage in off-site experiences and field work. Additions and refinements of plans are made as new information is discovered.

8. **Groups plan and prepare their reports**

   Pooling their findings and relating them to the initial questions, the group members develop a plan for creatively presenting their findings to the class. Visual and/or audio aids are chosen and tasks are assigned to develop scripts, posters, handouts, etc. Presentation is rehearsed.

9. **Groups present their findings to class**

   Using skits, panels, videos, etc., groups in turn present their findings in an interesting and effective way to the class.

10. **Class discusses the unit topic**

    Following group reports the entire class discusses findings, identifies major understandings, determines if their initial questions were answered.

11. **Plan and carry out a culminating activity.**

    To cement and celebrate their findings an activity is planned by which the class can share with other students, parents, and the community the results of their research and study. Appropriate action projects are planned and carried out.

12. **Class and teacher evaluate the experience**

    Students consider what they learned in terms of information, procedures, people, themselves. Teacher and students together evaluate the unit as a whole: What was successful? What improvements are needed? Teacher assesses student growth in knowledge, skill, values.

## Initiatory activities

Initiatory activities should catch students' attention, arouse questions, and give them a general idea of what the unit is all about. Saturating the environment with pertinent posters, displays, artifacts, music, etc., is a powerful way to set the stage for an exciting unit. An interdisciplinary team might work late on a Friday after school, creating an environment in team classrooms, hallways, and adjoining areas. It would leave no doubt that, beginning Monday morning, the focus is going to be on an issue such as "Nuclear Energy: Threat or Promise?"

Bulletin boards would carry posters from electric power companies extolling the virtues of nuclear power, contrasted with newspaper articles on the Chernobyl disaster and the world-wide anxiety it produced. Display cases might contain Geiger counters, samples of uranium-bearing rocks, and models of nuclear generating plants. Charts and graphs with statistics on the power potential of nuclear energy, predicted casualties from a nuclear attack, or the half-life of nuclear wastes would remind students that mathematical concepts also contribute to understanding the issue. Prominent in the environment would be pertinent books, including John Hersey's *Hiroshima* and various science fiction works on the possible fate of the world if nuclear energy is not wisely handled. In other words, everywhere a student looks there would be a reminder of the issue to be studied for the next week or two.

After students have had some time to experience the environment, the total group should be called together by the teacher or team to briefly overview the unit, establish ground rules, set a tentative timetable, and invite student questions and suggestions (Figure 10, Step 2). If possible, this meeting should be held in the team area, to capitalize on the environment, even if it means that students must sit on the floor in one of the classrooms or in the hallway. The meeting should be short and not get bogged down in details of requirements, deadlines, format of student projects, and the like. These details should be on a guide sheet given out and reviewed by individual teachers with smaller groups. In addition to a brief meeting to introduce the unit, the staff may want to invite in a dynamic visiting speaker or perhaps arrange a debate between proponents and opponents of nuclear energy. Sometimes a simulation or a short, hard-hitting film or videotape can dramatize the issues involved. It might even be possible to arrange a field trip to a museum or a nuclear power plant. All these, plus the more conventional orientation reading, introduce the students to the many ramifications of the unit (Figure 10, Step 3).

As soon as students have a general idea of the dimensions of the issue, they should identify specific sub-topics or problems that they would like to investigate in some depth (Figure 10, Step 4)

### Developmental activities

Investigations that make up the developmental phase of the unit may be carried out by students working alone, in pairs, or in small groups. Peer relationships are so important in the lives of middle level students that most work is best carried out by pairs or small groups. This enables them to develop interpersonal and social skills at the same time as they accomplish academic objectives.

Small group work sometimes is criticized as a waste of time, and, indeed, it can be if not properly managed. Both research (Slavin, 1991) and years of practical experience point to some key approaches that make it possible to capitalize on the tremendous potential of small group work while avoiding its many pitfalls. Among leading proponents of intelligently-managed group work are Johnson and Johnson (1987, 1990). Their wise suggestions include the necessity of establishing both individual accountability and total group responsibility for a project, report, or task. Evaluating both the work of the group and of each individual in the group is a first step. Students also need to be taught the skills of collaborative effort and not be allowed to flounder.

Even the question of how student groups should be formed (Figure 10, Step 5) has many different answers, depending upon one's educational objectives. If the primary goal is to examine the topic or issue, students should probably be asked to write on a slip of paper their first, second, and third choice of the subtopic they would like to study. The teacher arranges the groups, taking these preferences into account, but also seeks balance in group size, range of abilities, and other factors. On the other hand, for brief small group reactions to a speaker or film, random groupings formed by counting off are quickly assembled and give students an opportunity to work with different members of the class or team.

Sometimes it is desirable to have students choose the persons with whom they wish to work rather than the topic they prefer. This approach is appropriate when students are to carry out some task for the class. Students who are already friends can get down to work quickly, whereas strangers must first get acquainted and learn how to work together. The ultimate goal, of course, is for every member to be able and willing to work with any other classmate.

Asking students to list the people with whom they would like to work also provides the teacher with data on the social relations within the group. Such sociometric data can be of great benefit in counseling individual students, establishing subgroups for various activities, and managing the class. Middle level teachers are justifiably concerned about the cliques and isolates in their classes, but they may unwittingly make matters worse if they do not draw upon the time-tested wisdom of experts like Gronlund (1959).

The prevalence of small group work in interdisciplinary units should not obscure the need for other approaches. Occasional total-class or total-team lessons may be needed to provide important information on the topic under study, or students may need instruction in the skills of collaborative study, research, writing, calculating, or communicating the results of group work. Moreover, frequent progress reports to the entire group should be expected from each small group or pair, reinforcing the idea that the work is being done for the class or team, not just for the teachers.

Not to be overlooked, either, are the benefits of occasional individual investigations and presentations, as long as the same person is not always permitted to work alone. An individual project might be in order for a student who persistently shirks his or her responsibilities to a small group. On the other hand, a gifted student who feels held back by having to collaborate with others might, on occasion, be permitted to undertake a solo investigation (Vars and Rakow, in press).

Working in pairs also needs to be considered carefully. Some educators see this approach as a natural transition from the individual work typical of most school assignments to the desired small group work. With only two persons involved, decision-making is less complicated and dividing responsibilities is relatively easy. On the other hand, pairs have only each other to turn to for help and assistance, putting intense pressure on the relationship, whereas in a small group these are somewhat diffuse. Students working in pairs need help in how to function effectively, just as small groups do.

Students often need special help in "pooling" or synthesizing the information they have gathered and in preparing it for presentation to the class (Figure 10, Step 8). Too often each student in a group merely reports his or her findings, without regard for what others in the group have done. While teachers may want to examine each individual's notes as a measure of that person's effort, the final product should be a unitary work, whether it be a written report, a dramatic skit, a set of transparencies, video presentation, or whatever.

Student groups need access to a large chalkboard or bulletin board on which to arrange and re-arrange their ideas. Thumbtacks, tape, or slips from large "post-it" pads can be used for this purpose, or a bulletin board may be prepared with a spray that temporarily holds ordinary pieces of paper. An older technique is to construct a large "story board" or planning board, with pockets in which cards with key ideas can be placed and moved around as needed. In short, student groups, like teaching teams, need a visual record of plans as they develop.

Anyone who has sat through a series of typical oral reports knows how important it is that students be creative in their presentations (Figure 10, Step 9). With a little encouragement, students can come up with many different ways to share information. The instructional media used by teachers should be made available to students. Students often imitate popular television shows or commercials, with attention-getting results. Care must be taken, however, that the "message" does not get lost in the fun of designing an interesting "medium" of communication.

### Culminating activities

Individual and small group presentations, however informative and thought-provoking, must be fitted into the overall design of the interdisciplinary unit. General class discussion, additional total-class instruction by the teacher or team, and unit exams and evaluations all help keep student attention on the overall theme or issue (Figure 10, Steps 9-11). In addition, student learning can be shared with other classes in the building, or even with other schools. Videotapes, posters, and murals developed by the students might be displayed in a nearby shopping mall, and some of the student presentations might be shared "live" with parents and community members in an evening program. Preparing invitations and refreshments, decorating the meeting room or auditorium, greeting guests on the night of the performance — all these provide additional valuable learning experiences for students. Such events let the community know some of the good things going on in the schools, as a counter to the all-too-prevalent criticism.

Even more effective in culminating the unit is engaging students in some kind of action project. Action learning often is recommended for high school youth, but there are numerous instances of effective projects carried out by middle level students (Schine and Harrington, 1982; Rolzinski, 1990). For example, a middle school core class study of personal health and safety gained increased urgency when a student was injured at an unguarded crossing in front of the building. Students gathered data on auto and pedestrian traffic in the area and carried out a persistent campaign to get the city to place a guard at that crossing.

Likewise, a unit on ecology should stimulate efforts to preserve and enhance the environment, if only to launch a campaign to improve the school surroundings, to recycle waste paper, or to plant trees on the school grounds. In such projects, students might well join with adult public service groups seeking solutions to those problems, such as the Sierra Club, the Audubon Society, the Nature Conservancy, or the National Wildlife Federation. In a controversial issue like nuclear energy, with various pressure groups taking different positions, it may be best to encourage students to consider getting involved individually in the activities of the group of their choice. In any event, the message should be clear: young people and adults can and should work together to deal with the many social problems and issues that beset modern society (Lipka, Beane, O'Connell, 1985).

## EVALUATION

Evaluation of student progress is too complex a topic for adequate treatment in this monograph (see Vars, 1992b), but some of the special implications of interdisciplinary teaching must be considered. For example, if students conduct a small group investigation as part of a team-taught interdisciplinary unit, how does it "count" toward each student's grade? and in which subject or subjects? These complications must be addressed by the team *before* the unit is launched, or they will create countless headaches in the course of the unit.

If learning experiences are truly interdisciplinary, assigning separate grades for each subject area is likely to be arbitrary, at best. This being the case, one teacher engaged his students in cooperatively deciding which activities would be "counted" toward which subject. All the activities carried out during the marking period were listed on the chalkboard, and teacher and students decided together which would be considered as English, which social studies, and which science. In keeping with the spirit of the class, each student then wrote a memo to the teacher and to his or her parents indicating what grade he or she felt would be fair and why. The teacher added comments, and this memo was sent home with the official report card.

The broader the goals of an interdisciplinary program, the more inadequate is the typical A-B-C mark. If the program is designed to promote problem-solving, interpersonal skills, and leadership, it is just as important to report progress on these as on the acquisition of content. At the very least, interdisciplinary teachers should supplement the conventional report card with checklists, anecdotal memos, samples of student work, and student self-evaluations. Figure 11 contains excerpts from an extensive five page self-evaluation used in a ninth grade core class in Lexington, Kentucky. Other examples may be found in the landmark book by Zapf listed in the references.

In view of the lack of fit between the usual A-B-C marking system and the broad purposes of middle level education (Vars, 1983), some schools have revamped their entire marking and reporting system. A rationale, case study, and sample evaluation forms used in one such school were described by Vars in 1982. Schools must continuously scrutinize and revise their procedures for evaluating and reporting student progress, for these reveal very clearly what is really valued by the school staff, all rhetoric and high-sounding school philosophy aside.

# Figure 11

# Student Self-evaluation of Progress in Core

**Nine Weeks**
**Evaluation**

Name _____

Date _____ Section ___

As we began our year together, we lifted up certain principles and goals for our core experience this year. To indicate where you are now, please place a check on the line for each question below and describe your position in words in the space below.

1. "In core we care about you." To what degree do you care about the rest of us in this group?

I care only about myself.                                    Others' good is my
To heck with the others.                                        chief concern.

2. To what degree do you feel we care about *you*?

I feel completely alone,                              I feel loved and accepted
ignored, misunderstood in here.                    by everyone at all times
                                                                        in this class.

3. To what degree do you think you have changed (learned):
   in knowing? (knowledge, new information)

I haven't found out                                              I feel full of
any new information.                                          many new facts.

   in feeling? (awareness of self and others; change in attitudes)

I'm still the old me —                                    A whole new attitude
my feelings are the same as always.              toward people and learn-
                                                                  ing has opened up to me.

   in doing? (actions, behavior)

I see no change in my behavior                    I see myself freed to do
from last year or even yesterday.                  acceptable things I
                                                              never dreamed I could.

4. What do you think about the atmosphere for learning (discipline) in our classroom?

| Too much control | Love and control in balance | Too much love (caring) |
| --- | --- | --- |

5. In group discussion, your own participation is:

| Zero. I say nothing. Others' words don't touch me. | I talk all the time, contributing great ideas. |
| --- | --- |

6. Where do you rate your listening skills?

| I am not tuned in but am shut up and refuse to hear anyone or anything. | I listen carefully, with my ears, my mind, and my cmotions to both verbal and non-verbal communications. |
| --- | --- |

7. In group work your participation is:

| Completely irresponsible. | Perfect. I listen, contribute, am responsible. |
| --- | --- |

8. Where are you in your project?

| I haven't done a thing. | I know all there is to know about it and have a perfect report to give. |
| --- | --- |

9. If learning is change in knowing, feeling, and doing, and if our emphasis is on the process of becoming more than on the accumulation of facts, and if you feel you are not the same person who came here at the start of the year, how would you rate yourself in your own growth, efforts, and changes?

| F | D | C | B | A |
| --- | --- | --- | --- | --- |

## CONCLUSION/SUMMARY

Interdisciplinary units provide unparalleled opportunities to involve students directly in the learning process. This is essential in teaching at any level, but it is especially important in the middle grades. Students should play a vital role in creating both the physical and the emotional climate for learning in the classroom. Once the teacher or team has captured student interest through well-chosen initiatory activities, students should share in formulating specific questions for study and then bear most of the responsibility for seeking answers, preferably in carefully-guided small groups. Group presentations are followed by culminating activities, to tie the unit experiences together and lead students to carry their conclusions into some socially-responsible action. Students also should be involved in evaluating all aspects of the interdisciplinary unit and should share in communicating to parents and others the quality of their learning. While none of these techniques is unique to interdisciplinary teaching, their application to significant interdisciplinary topics or issues gives them enhanced effectiveness.

# 5.

## Skill Development

Basic learning and thinking skills are essential in mastering the content of any subject area, whether or not it is absorbed into an interdisciplinary unit. This can be demonstrated by charting skill objectives in the various subjects included in an interdisciplinary program, as illustrated in Figure 12. With such a chart before them, an interdisciplinary team can choose one team member who can best provide instruction in a certain skill. This person might introduce the skill to the entire student group at one time, with all team members following up and helping students apply the skill in their respective classes. Or each team member may decide to develop that skill in his or her unique way. In either case, when every member of an interdisciplinary team calls attention to the importance of a certain skill, the students are bound to get the message.

Interdisciplinary instruction also creates opportunities to demonstrate the importance of skills that students too often view as meaningless. For example, isolated drill on reading speed and comprehension, while necessary, achieves validity when students use those skills to obtain information they want to learn. Moreover, students will work their way through reading material presumably far above their reading level if they need the information. They can see that accuracy in spelling and writing is essential in a letter sent to the editor of the local paper, in contrast with something merely turned in to the teacher for a grade. Interpersonal skills are refined daily in various types of cooperative learning, and higher order thinking skills are learned through tackling real problems, not doing contrived exercises in a workbook. The functional application of all kinds of skills is a major value of the interdisciplinary approach.

# Figure 12

## Excerpt from "Shared Objectives" Grade 8, Hampton City Schools

| GRADE 8 | ENGLISH | SOCIAL STUDIES | READING | LIBRARY | MATH | SCIENCE |
|---|---|---|---|---|---|---|
| Organizing information by classifying. | The student will classify characters, plots, themes, styles of writing; classify information into main and subordinate ideas; distinguish between fact and fiction. | Classify pictures, facts, and events under main headings or in categories. | The student will identify the author's organization of materials (classification, sequence, comparison - contrast). | | The student will identify polygons given specified characteristics. | The student will identify characteristics and examples of various types of matter by their physical and chemical properties. |
| Acquiring information through reading. | Continued emphasis on wide reading for pleasure; plus reading that leads to a better understanding of self, others, and the trials and triumphs of life. | A.Skim to find a particular word, get a general impression, or locate specific information. B. Read to find answers to questions. C. Make use of headings, topic sentences, and summary sentences to select main idea and differentiate between main and subordinate ideas. D. Select the statements that are pertinent to the topic being studied. E. Consciously evaluate what is read. | Scan content for answers to specific questions or problems. Skim content to survey for main ideas and topics. | The student will recognize and obtain information from specialized dictionaries. | The student will read to determine the facts and the question in word problems. | The student will use process skills as a basis for defining and solving problems and answering questions related to the study of the physicval environment. |

Source:  A Guide for Team Planning: Middle School Level. (1984).  Hampton VA: Hampton City Schools, pp. 54-55

Merely using those skills is not sufficient, however. Students must have the skills brought to their attention, so that they will understand why time is set aside for specific practice. An obvious example is spelling. In addition to the basic list of spelling and vocabulary words that may be designated for the grade level, words encountered in the interdisciplinary unit should be incorporated in the weekly spelling lesson (Vars, 1987). Problems in grammar, usage, and syntax encountered in the unit should be used to provide motivation and practice in specific periods set aside for English. An English teacher who has twenty-five examples from student papers of their incorrect punctuation of possessive nouns does not have to argue the point. He or she may merely flash the mistakes on the overhead projector (without student names, of course), and engage the students in the task of figuring out what is wrong and how the problem can be solved.

Skill development both within the interdisciplinary unit and in separate but related instructional periods may be easily managed by a block-time or self-contained class teacher. With an interdisciplinary team it takes joint planning.

Some teams assign year-long responsibility for certain types of skills. For example, the science teacher on the team may monitor the development of decision-making skills, provide direct instruction within the classes he or she teaches, and point out to the entire staff and student body where critical decision-making takes place in the course of the unit. The social studies teacher might assume responsibility for such skills as map reading, use of documents, and interviewing. The mathematics teacher, in addition to such expected responsibilities as interpreting charts and transforming mathematical data into graphic form, might help students learn how to search computer data bases and to use the computer to prepare data for display. The English teacher on the team may monitor and teach the language and reference skills ordinarily associated with the field. Care must be taken that such a division does not result in either teachers or students assuming, for example, that writing is being taught only by the English teacher or that decision-making is something we do only with the science teacher. In a truly interdisciplinary unit, all teachers assume responsibility for all skills, even though they have primary responsibility for certain ones.

As an alternative to assigning skills to different members of the team, some staff prefer to emphasize particular skills in certain interdisciplinary units. For example, a unit on environmental pollution, involving field study of pollution levels in local streams, would seem the natural place to stress careful data gathering, preparing charts and tables, and application of elementary statistical analysis to interpret the results. Skills of this type would be brought out by all members of the team during such a unit. On the other hand, a unit on the multicultural roots of people in the community would be the obvious time to stress interpretation of original documents, interviewing people with different cultural backgrounds, and interpreting data in verbal rather than mathematical form. Of course, deciding to emphasize certain skills in a particular unit does not mean that teachers ignore them all the rest of the year; but highlighting certain skills at different points of the year is more effective than merely resolving to stress a certain skill "all year." Teachers usually have too many things to keep in mind as it is, so a vague, year-long intention is likely to get lost (Rapp, 1986).

Some middle schools or teams also establish a "skill of the week" schedule for the entire staff to follow. The skill is announced at the beginning of the week and addressed by every member of the staff at some point in the week's instruction. While this approach lacks the direct relationship between a skill and its functional use in a meaningful interdisciplinary unit, it does have added impact because all or nearly all of the staff point out its relevance in their courses. The total staff should be involved in deciding the skill to be emphasized each week, with an effort to select those most widely applicable to all fields of study. Thinking skills and interpersonal skills are prime candidates for such a list.

A total-school approach also may be effective with vocabulary and spelling words, as a supplement to the learning embedded within an interdisciplinary unit. The "word for the day" may be announced in the morning, with a prize for the first student who submits an accurate definition, explanation, and an example of its use in a sentence that would be understood by other students; or every staff member may attempt to incorporate the word in class instruction that day, pointing out its relevance to whatever topic is under study. Language is so vital to learning that schools need to use many means to stimulate its development.

Students and teachers know that they are in school to learn "the basic skills," but sometimes the less conventional skills are overlooked. For example, in an interdisciplinary unit utilizing small groups, direct attention should be focused on the processes of group work in addition to the product. The duties of such group officers as chairman, recorder, and process observer should be listed, discussed, and perhaps demonstrated by one of the small groups. Groups might role-play alternative ways to deal with an overbearing group member or one who fails to carry a proper share of the load. Conflict resolution can be demonstrated, as well as specific techniques for ensuring that the contributions of all group members are incorporated in the final product.

Similarly, thinking and decision-making skills should be developed, both through use and through direct instruction. Ackerman and Perkins (1989) have pointed out differences between content-oriented and skills-oriented integration of subject matter. They urged educators to develop a "metacurriculum" of thinking and learning skills and described several ways to integrate this curriculum with content. A number of authorities have proposed ways to teach thinking skills "across the curriculum" (Swartz and Perkins, 1990).

Research on methods of teaching also yields useful suggestions. For example, inquiry strategies are directly applicable in a problem-centered interdisciplinary unit, and debriefing thinking processes is a key feature of these approaches. Especially important in dealing with controversial issues is the role of values in decision-making. Kirschenbaum (1992) offers many wise suggestions for negotiating this sensitive area without succumbing to either value neutrality or indoctrination.

In short, good interdisciplinary teaching helps students meaningfully to integrate content and a variety of skills — learning, thinking, and interpersonal. Both teachers and students should periodically step back from their work on a unit to ask themselves such questions as: "How are we doing?" "How can we improve our procedures for working together?" "How can each of us make a better contribution to the group effort?" "How can we improve our decision-making?" "What learning skills need refinement?" Posing questions like these in the classroom provides a constant reminder of important goals too often overlooked in the usual emphasis on academic skills.

## SUMMARY

In summary, skill development within an interdisciplinary unit employs many of the techniques used by effective teachers in all subjects but relates them to the problem or topic under study. Skills taught as applied are learned more effectively and are more likely to be carried over into real life. Moreover, an interdisciplinary unit makes it possible to stress thinking and interpersonal skills that are too often overlooked in conventional instruction.

# 6.

## Teacher Guidance

Young people going through the transition years have a tremendous need for guidance. They have countless questions and concerns about their changing bodies, their changing social relations with peers and adults, and the many critical decisions typically made during these years concerning smoking, drugs, alcohol, sex, and careers, to name only a few. It has been truly said that a person's character is very largely formed by the time he or she emerges from early adolescence. The middle school years are quite literally the last time that parents and teachers are likely to have a major influence on moral values and life-style.

Middle level schools address this need in several ways. Most schools of any size have at least one guidance counselor who coordinates the efforts of teachers, administrators, and other staff. Unfortunately, with student-to-counselor ratios as high as 400 to one, only students in very serious trouble are likely to receive professional guidance services.

Many middle schools have a teacher-advisory program, in which groups of students meet with a designated teacher to deal with concerns typical of the age group (Cole, 1992). The teacher-advisor also usually monitors the student's academic progress and maintains contact with the home. Staff members who are adequately prepared for this role and committed to it provide a vital service for students. Unfortunately, when either of these conditions is absent, students may not receive the attention they need. In order to hold advisory groups to a reasonable size, it is necessary for nearly every staff member to have a group. This virtually guarantees that some groups will be assigned to staff members who are not enthusiastic about this responsibility.

Schools with block-time or self-contained programs often include guidance as part of the homeroom or home-base responsibilities of these teachers. The argument is that these teachers get to know their students especially well, since they have them in class several periods a day. Moreover, the longer block of time enables the teacher to "work in" guidance sessions as they are needed, instead of being locked into a specific time or day of the week. Since guidance is an essential element of the core concept, teachers of this special kind of block-time program nearly always assume this responsibility, and core units normally deal directly with areas of student concern, such as personal health, drugs, interpersonal relations, careers, and the like. It also is expected that the core teacher will develop close, cooperative relationships with parents, making guidance still more effective.

In block-time or self-contained arrangements, teacher guidance is in the hands of a relatively small number of staff members who presumably know the students well and have enough time to deal with these matters as appropriate. These advantages tend to offset the fact that such teachers work with regular-size classroom groups, rather than the 12 to 15 students typical of advisory groups (Vars, 1989).

Guidance also can be provided indirectly through interdisciplinary units of study. Units such as the study of other cultures can serve a guidance function if they include consideration of how young people live and negotiate adolescence in other nations. For example, study of courting customs in Latin America could lead naturally to consideration of the nature of dating in our culture, what is and is not appropriate behavior, the importance of sensitivity and concern for others, and the like. Hardships faced by the pioneers and experienced vicariously by students through a simulation lead naturally to consideration of the "hardships" young people face growing up today. Through literature students can enter into the lives of others, both real and fictional, to see how they dealt with life's problems. In short, nearly any interdisciplinary unit can help young people grapple with their personal concerns if at least a portion of the study is approached through the perspective of the young.

Better yet, units may be open-ended enough to allow direct student input through teacher-student planning to decide on topics or questions for study. The unit itself may be chosen through teacher-student planning, once the assigned problem area has been previewed. Under these circumstances, guidance and curriculum are merged.

The methods used in interdisciplinary units also can serve guidance objectives. Class discussion of issues significant to young people may reassure individuals that they are not the only ones with certain worries or concerns. An especially potent method is small group work, where students develop interpersonal relations even as they learn skills and investigate a topic or issue. Group membership should change frequently, so students learn to work with different kinds of people. Students also learn about their own strengths and weaknesses as they fill various roles in the group process. Skits and role-playing enable students to "try on" different personalities. Journal-keeping and expressive writing enable each young person to deal with feelings and to wrestle with personal moral choices. Methods that challenge students to seek the personal meaning of their experiences and to explore wholesome ways of interacting with peers and adults can be significant guidance tools. When either the content or the methods of an interdisciplinary unit touch on guidance matters, there is a natural bridge to the teacher-advisory program. Issues raised in the course of the unit can be brought up for more intensive discussion in the guidance or advisory group. For example, sixth grade interdisciplinary teams at Cosburn Middle School in Toronto, Ontario, organize their program around three major themes: Change, Survival, and Fantasy. The following introduction to the first section of the Change unit points out the connections between the interdisciplinary unit and the advisor/advisee program:

> This section provides students with opportunities to explore their own personal experiences and to begin to collect and analyze data for use in later sections. Its activities combine the learning of certain geographical concepts (e.g., locality, land use, climate) and certain scientific concepts (that many of our activities — daily, monthly, yearly — are controlled by movements of the earth and moon). Some health concepts (changes associated with puberty) are integrated in the section as well as the application of basic concepts of the Math Programme. A number of the activities in the section are an integral part of the Advisor/Advisee programme (Cosburn Middle School, 1984).

Guidance functions should not be limited to classroom teachers or official group advisors, of course. A question/suggestion box prominently displayed in any classroom throughout the year is an excellent way of soliciting student concerns for discussion in guidance sessions. The question box also can be used by a student to request a personal conference with the teacher.

## CONCLUSION

An interdisciplinary unit can serve as an excellent vehicle for providing guidance through content, methods, specific guidance sessions, and personal teacher-student conferences, all supervised and coordinated by the professional guidance staff.

# 7.

## Resources

Interdisciplinary teaching makes enormous demands on teachers if it is done properly. Therefore everyone involved should help muster all available resources. The most important resource is people — library/media specialists, other teachers and staff members, parents, community members, and the students themselves. A middle school media staff can help greatly by maintaining a community resources file, with names, addresses, and telephone numbers of people who are willing to serve as resources of one kind or another. Also needed is a listing of places suitable for field trips. In some schools, these files are maintained by parent volunteers, who periodically circulate questionnaires to staff, parents, and the community at large. Too often overlooked is the resourcefulness of the students themselves, especially when they see the value of the study. The Foxfire project has amply demonstrated how older youth can tap community resources (Wigginton, 1985). With adequate supervision, middle level students can do likewise. This was demonstrated in the oral history project carried out in the John Read Middle School, Redding, Connecticut. Students demonstrated maturity and competence in interviewing elderly citizens, preparing reports, and contributing to the community's understanding of its past (Fuerst and Loh, 1986).

Interdisciplinary units also draw upon a great variety of instructional materials and combine them in ways that cross the boundaries of the usual library filing system. A group researching an environmental issue will find pertinent references under science, history, sociology, political science, health, and many other areas. Videotapes, computer data banks, films, sound filmstrips, packaged simulations, cassette tapes, models, and posters all must be located, studied, evaluated, and integrated into the examination of the issue. Media centers are really the hub of the action in schools where interdisciplinary teaching is taking place.

To supplement the resources provided by the school media center, interdisciplinary teams or block-time teachers probably will want to develop their own collections of materials especially pertinent to their particular approach to a topic or issue. The microcomputer can be a valuable tool in keeping track of these materials. McElwain (1986) found in her work in Highland Middle School, Barberton, Ohio, that materials, activities, and resources could easily be edited, updated, and organized by means of a computerized resource unit.

Teachers also may find that the resource folder system is a suitable way of keeping track of instructional materials filed in the classroom (Vars, 1961). This system consists of a manila folder for each interdisciplinary unit, in which are listed the titles and locations of related materials. The materials themselves are placed on shelves or in files alphabetically. Any one item may be listed in several different resource folders, where appropriate.

Teachers or teams inevitably develop interdisciplinary units in their own unique ways, but they can benefit from examining units developed by others. Teachers are urged to keep informed of new developments through reading professional journals and attending workshops and conferences.

A few sources especially appropriate for middle grades teachers are described below.

**1.  National Association for Core Curriculum, 404 White Hall, Kent State University, Kent, OH 44242-0001.** Units of various lengths are sold at cost. New units are announced in the Association's quarterly newsletter, *The Core Teacher*. Write for current list. Titles currently available include the following:

> "Creating Our Own Society," by Rosita Jimenez, Theresa Kinealy, Eva Horan, John Dinan, and Karen Miller, Denver Public Schools, 1988 .

> "What on Earth? A Cross-Curricular Unit on the Environment," by Susan Morice and Susan O'Grady, Wydown Middle School, Clayton, MO, 1990.

"The Return of the Bald Eagle," by Sam Lewbel and Linda Gejda, Rochambeau Middle School, Southbury, CT, 1991 .

"The Civil War: An Interdisciplinary Unit for Eighth Grade Social Studies and English," by Bill Clark, West Muskingum Middle School, Zanesville, OH, 1987.

2.   **National Resource Center for Middle Grades Education, University of South Florida, 4207 Fowler Avenue, Tampa, FL 33620-5620.** Thematic/interdisciplinary units for upper elementary and middle grades students available for purchase. Recent titles include: "Ants and More Ants," "Our Prehistoric Ancestors," "Pirates of Old," "Dragons," and "Time on the Line." Write for current list.

3.   **ERIC Document Reproduction Service, Cincinnati Bell Information Systems, 7420 Fullerton Road, Suite 110, Springfield, VA 22153-2853.** Units occasionally appear in this source and are available in either microfiche or photocopy form. Titles are listed in *Resources in Education,* under the descriptor "Teaching Guides." The following interdisciplinary guide was announced in a recent issue:

"Alaska Wildlife Week - Junior/Senior High School Teacher's Guide, Unit 7. Together we can help wildlife," ED 340 573. Alaska State Department of Fish and Game, Division of Wildlife Conservation.

A variety of activities are included to help secondary students understand which human activities help wildlife and which harm wildlife...Suggestions on planning hands-on projects to improve wildlife habitat or to become involved in decision-making about Alaska wildlife are included...The four lessons included in this guide contain background information for teachers, introductory activities, and ideas for curriculum integration.

Similar guides are available for primary teachers and upper elementary teachers.

**4.   Association for Supervision and Curriculum Development, 1250 North Pitt Street, Alexandria, VA 22314-1403.** Resource units and interdisciplinary units occasionally appear among the curriculum materials displayed at the annual ASCD convention. These are listed in the curriculum display bibliography for that year, along with the source and cost, if available. Some interdisciplinary units listed in recent years include: "Futuristics." Anne Arundel County, MD, 1982; "Asian and African Culture." Yonkers Public Schools, NY, 1985.

**5.   University of Northern Colorado, Middle Level Interdisciplinary Education Center, McKee Hall, Room 213, Greeley, CO 80637.** More than 75 units available at minimal cost, some more fully developed than others. Write for current list.

**6.   Other sources.** Teaching units and resource guides sometimes appear in textbooks on curriculum or teaching methods. Here are a few recent examples:

> "Living in the Future," an illustrative interdisciplinary resource unit found in *Curriculum Planning and Development* by James A. Beane, Conrad F. Toepfer, Jr., and Samuel J. Alessi (Boston: Allyn and Bacon, 1986, pp. 401-417). Includes: Rationale Statement, Objectives, Content, Activities (keyed to the objectives), Resources, Measuring Devices, Self-evaluation, and a description of the "jigsaw method" of cooperative learning.

> "Energy," is one of a number of thematic unit plans included in *Interdisciplinary Methods: A Thematic Approach* by Alan H. Humphreys, Thomas R. Post, and Arthur K. Ellis (Santa Monica, CA: Goodyear, 1981, pp. 112-148). This unit includes a webbing diagram of the unit, introduction, unit objectives, appropriate grade levels and 23 activities. Each activity lists specific objectives, materials, and evaluation suggestions. Most units in this book are brief and aimed at grades three through six, but they could be adapted for other middle grades classes.

*Interdisciplinary Units in New England's Middle
Schools: A How-To Guide,* (1989) and *What and Why?*
(1991). These two useful monographs by Sam Lewbel
describe a variety of interdisciplinary units and set them
in theoretical context. Available from the New England
League of Middle Schools, 460 Boston Street, Suite 4,
Topsfield, MA 01983.

# 8.

---

# Summary and Conclusion

---

S ince life itself is "interdisciplinary," at least some portion of the school curriculum should also be interdisciplinary if it is to help young people relate to life. This monograph described ways that middle school teachers may provide effective interdisciplinary instruction. Approaches include the single teacher, the interdisciplinary team, and the correlated, fused, or core approach to curriculum. Interdisciplinary units may be planned by charting content or objectives, webbing, mapping out broad problem areas, or engaging students in open-ended teacher-student planning.

Effective interdisciplinary units may be launched by immersing students in a stimulating environment and providing them with a unit overview. Developmental activities ordinarily include small group work and culminating activities in which students tie all the threads together, share their findings with others, and perhaps carry some of them into action projects. In addition to the conventional report card, a variety of other procedures are needed to evaluate and report the many kinds of student progress evident in an interdisciplinary unit.

Interdisciplinary units provide an excellent vehicle for functional application of a variety of skills, but skill development must be carefully planned and monitored. Likewise, teacher guidance may be inherent in both the content and the methods employed in the unit, but small group sessions and individual conferences also are needed. Teachers must mobilize a variety of resources to carry out interdisciplinary teaching.

Interdisciplinary teaching is no easy task, but its rewards for both students and teachers are impressive. Middle level students need ample opportunities to experience the connectedness of things through the study of well-planned and executed interdisciplinary units.

## REFERENCES

Ackerman, D. & Perkins, D. C. (1989). Integrating thinking and learning skills across the curriculum. In H. H. Jacobs (Ed.), *Interdisciplinary curriculum: Design and implementation,* pp. 77-95. Alexandria, VA: Association for Supervision and Curriculum Development.

Alexander, W. M. et al. (1968). *The emergent middle school.* NY: Holt, Rinehart, and Winston.

American Association for the Advancement of Science. (1989). *Science for all Americans.* Washington, D.C: The Association.

Arhar, J. M., Johnston, J. H., and Markle, G. C. (1992). The effects of teaming and collaborative arrangements. The effects of teaming on students. In J. H. Lounsbury (Ed.), *Connecting the curriculum throuqh interdisciplinary instruction,* pp. 15-22, 23-35. Columbus, OH: National Middle School Association.

Aspy, D. N. and Roebuck, F. N. (1977). *Kids don't learn from people they don't like.* Amherst, MA: Human Resource Development Press.

Beane, J. A. (1976). "Options for interdisciplinary teams." *Dissemination Services On the Middle Grades, 7*(5), 1-4.

Beane, J. A. (1992). *Exploring middle school curriculum options.* Madison, WI: Wisconsin Public Television. (Three videotapes.)

Beane, J. A. (1993). *A middle school curriculum: From rhetoric to reality* (2nd ed.). Columbus, OH: National Middle School Association.

Bergmann, S.K. (1986). Guidance in interdisciplinary programs. *Transescence, 14* (1), 22-25.

Brady, M. (1989). *What's worth teaching? Selecting, organizing. and integrating knowledge.* Albany, NY: State University of New York Press.

Brady, M. (1991). The here and now as curriculum. *Transescence, 19* (1), 27-32.

Brennan, P. and Alessi, R. (1981). *American Studies at Central Junior High School, Greenwich, Connecticut.* Kent, OH: National Association for Core Curriculum.

Brodhagen, B., Weilbacher, G. and Beane, J. (1992). Living in the future: An experiment with an integrated curriculum. *Dissemination services on the middle grades, 23* (9), 1-7.

Caine, R. N. and Caine, G. (1991). *Making connections: Teaching and the human brain.* Alexandria, VA: Association for Supervision and Curriculum Development.

Carnegie Council on Adolescent Development. (1989). *Turning Points: Preparing American youth for the 21st century.* NY: Carnegie Corporation of New York.

Carr, J., Eppig, P., and Monether, P. (1986). Learning by solving real problems. *Middle School Journal, 17* (2), 14-16.

Cheek, D. W. (1992). *Thinking constructively about science, technology and society.* Albany, NY: State University of New York Press.

Cole, C. (1992). *Nurturing a teacher advisory program.* Columbus, OH: National Middle School Association.

Cosburn Middle School. (1984). *Change.* Toronto, Ontario: Board of Education, Borough of East York.

Curriculum Task Force of the National Commission on Social Studies in the Schools. (1989). *Charting the course: Social studies for the 21st century.* Washington, DC: The Commission.

Davies, M. A. (1992). Are interdisciplinary units worthwhile? Ask students. In J. H. Lounsbury (Ed.), *Connecting the curriculum throuqh interdisciplinary instruction,* pp. 37-41. Columbus, OH: National Middle School Association.

Eichhorn, D. H. (1966). *The middle school.* NY: Center for Applied Research in Education. (Reissued in 1987 by National Middle School Association, Columbus, OH)

Erb, T. and Doda, N. (1989). *Team organization: Promise, practice and possibilities.* Washington, DC.: National Education Association.

Fogarty, R. (1991). *The mindful school: How to integrate the curricula.* Glen Elyn, IL: Skylight Publishing.

Froese, V. (Ed.). (1991). *Whole-language: Practice and theory.* Boston: Allyn and Bacon.

Fuerst, D. and Loh, A. (1986). Creating an oral history project. *Middle School Journal, 17* (2), 10-13.

Gehrke, N. J. (1991). Beyond the terrestrial: A schema for integrative curriculum. *Transescence, 19* (1), 38-43.

George, P. S. and Alexander, W. M. (1993). *The exemplary middle school,* (2nd ed.). New York: Harcourt, Brace, Jovanovich.

Gronlund, N. (1959). *Sociometry in the classroom.* New York: Harper.

Gruhn, W.T. and Douglass, H.R. (1947). *The Modern Junior High School.* NY: Ronald Press.

Harnack, R. (1965). Computer based resource units. *Educational Leadership, 23,* 239-245.

Hart, L. (1983). *Human brain and human learning.* NY: Longman.

Humphrey, A., Post, T., and Ellis, A. (1981). *Interdisciplinary methods: A thematic approach.* Santa Monica, CA: Goodyear.

Jacobs, H. H. (Ed.). (1989). *Interdisciplinary curriculum: Design and implementation.* Alexandria, VA: Association for Supervision and Curriculum Development.

Jardine, D. W. (1991). On the integrity of things: Ecopodagogical reflections on the integrated curriculum. *Transescence, 19* (1), 33-37.

Johnson, D. W. and Johnson, R. J. (1987). *Learning together and alone: Cooperation, competition, and individualization,* (2nd ed.). Englewood Cliffs, NJ: Prentice-Hall.

Johnson, D. W., Johnson, R. J., and Holubec, E. J. (1990). *Circles of learning: Cooperation in the classroom,* (3rd ed.). Edina, MN: Interaction Book Company.

Kerekes, J. (1987). The interdisciplinary unit — it's here to stay. *Middle School Journal, 18* (4), 12-14.

Kirschenbaum, H. (1992). A comprehensive model for values education and moral education. *Educational Leadership, 73* (10), 771-776.

Levy, P. S. (1980). Webbing: A format for planning integrated curricula. *Middle School Journal, 11* (3), 26-27.

Lipka, R. P., Beane, J. A., and O'Connell, B. (1985). *Community service projects.* Bloomington, IN: Phi Delta Kappa Foundation.

Lounsbury, J. H. and Vars, G. F. (1978). *A curriculum for the middle school years.* New York: Harper.

Lounsbury, J. H. (Ed.). (1992). *Connecting the curriculum through interdisciplinary instruction.* Columbus, OH: National Middle School Association.

McElwain, D. (1986). *A computerized resource unit.* Barberton, OH: the author.

Merenbloom, E. Y. (1991). *The team process in the middle school: A handbook for teachers,* (3rd ed.). Columbus, OH: National Middle School Association.

Merenbloom, E. Y. (1986). The interdisciplinary team approach. *Transescence, 14* (1), 6-11.

Miller, R. (1992). *What are schools for? Holistic education in American culture,* (2nd ed.). Brandon, VT: Holistic Education Press.

National Council of Teachers of Mathematics. (1989). *Curriculum and evaluation standards for school mathematics.* Washington, D.C.: National Council of Teachers of Mathematics.

Orange County Public Schools. (1982). *Intermediate education team guidelines/strategies.* Orlando, FL: The Schools.

Perkins, D. N. (1989). Selecting fertile themes for integrated learning. In H. H. Jacobs (Ed.), *Interdisciplinary curriculum: Design and implementation,* pp. 67-76. Alexandria, VA: Association for Supervision and Curriculum Development.

Rapp, R. (1986). Developing basic skills in an interdisciplinary program. *Transescence, 14* (1), 17-21.

Resources for Youth. (1981). *New roles for early adolescents.* Boston, MA: Resources for Youth, Inc.

Rogers, C. (1968). *The interpersonal relationship in the facilitation of learning.* Columbus, OH: Charles E. Merrill.

Rolzinski, C. A. (1990). *The adventure of adolescence: Middle school students and community service.* Washington, D.C.: Youth Service America.

Schine, J. G. and Harrington, D. (1982). *Youth participation for early adolescents.* Fastback 174. Bloomington, IN: Phi Delta Kappa.

Slavin, R. E. (1990). *Cooperative learninq: Theory, research. and practice.* Englewood Cliffs, NJ: Prentice-Hall.

Slavin, R. E. (1991). Synthesis of research on cooperative learning. *Educational Leadership, 48* (5), 71-82.

Stanford, G. (1977). *Developing effective classroom groups: A practical guide for teachers.* New York: Hart Publishing Company.

Stewart, W. J. (1982). *Transforming traditional unit teaching.* Boston, MA: American Press.

Stromberg, R. and Smith, J. (1987). The simulation technique—applied in an Ancient Egypt I.D.U. *Middle School Journal, 18* (4), 9-11.

Swartz, R. J. and Perkins, D. N. (1990). *Teaching thinking: Issues and approaches.* Pacific Grove, CA: Midwest Publishing.

Van Til, W., Vars, G. F., and Lounsbury, J. H. (1967). *Modern education for the junior high school years* (2nd ed.). Indianapolis: Bobbs-Merrill.

Van Til, W. (1976). What should be taught and learned through secondary education? In W. Van Til (Ed.), *Issues in secondary education,* pp. 196-212. 75th yearbook of the National Society for the Study of Education. Chicago: University of Chicago Press.

Vars, A. M. (1986). Focus on relationships. *Transescence, 14* (1), 26-31.

Vars, G. F. (1961). Organizing instructional materials for teaching core. *High School Journal, 44* (7), 232-238.

Vars, G. F. (Ed.). (1969). *Common learnings: Core and interdisciplinary team approaches.* Scranton, PA: Intext.

Vars, G. F. (1979). Fire protection for innovative programs. *Educational Leadership, 37* (3), 221-224.

Vars, G. F. (1982). *Evaluating and reporting student progress in the middle school: A case study and teachers' manual.* Kent, OH: Cricket Press.

Vars, G. F. (1983). Missiles, marks, and the middle level student. *NASSP Bulletin, 67,* 72-77.

Vars, G. F. (1984). The functions of middle level schools. In J. H. Lounsbury (Ed.), *Perspectives: Middle school education 1964-1984,* pp. 39-51. Columbus, OH: National Middle School Association.

Vars, G. F. (Ed.). (1986a). Integrating the middle grades curriculum. (Special Issue.) *Transescence, 14* (1), 3-31.

Vars, G. F. (1986b). Block-time and core approaches. *Transescence, 14* (1), 12-16.

Vars, G. F. (1987). On their own in spelling. *The Educational Oasis, 3* (1), 17-18.

Vars, G. F. (January, 1989). Getting closer to middle level students: options for teacher-adviser guidance programs. *Schools in the middle: A report on trends and practices.* Washington, D.C.: National Association of Secondary School Principals.

Vars, G. F. (1991). *A bibliography of research on the effectiveness of block-time. core, and interdisciplinary team teaching programs.* Kent, OH: National Association for Core Curriculum.

Vars, G. F. (1992a). Integrative curriculum: A déjà vu. *Current Issues in Middle Level Education, 1* (1), 66-78.

Vars, G. F. (1992b). Humanizing student evaluation and reporting. In Judith Irvin, (Ed.), *Transforming middle level education,* pp. 336-365. Boston: Allyn and Bacon.

Vars, G. F. and Rakow, S. R. (In press). Making connections: Integrative curriculum and the gifted student. *Roeper Review.*

Wigginton, E. (1985). *Sometimes a shining moment: The Foxfire experience.* Garden City, NY: Anchor Press/Doubleday.

Wright, G. S. (1949). *Core curriculum in public high schools: An inquiry into practices, 1949.* Bulletin 1950, No. 5. Washington, D.C.: U.S. Office of Education.

Zapf, R. (1959). *Democratic processes in the secondary classroom.* Englewood Cliffs, NJ: Prentice-Hall.